W9-CGP-614

EILEEN GEORGE'S

CONVERSATIONS IN HEAVEN
II

THE MEET-THE-FATHER MINISTRY, Inc.
363 Greenwood St.
Millbury, MA 01527

Library of Congress Catalog Card Number 94-75689

ISBN 0-9624588-3-X Volume Two 10.00

Imprimatur: Most Reverend Timothy J. Harrington, D.D.
Bishop of Worcester
December 6, 1993

The Imprimatur of the Bishop is not a judgment that the contents of the
book are of supernatural origin, nor that it is free from error. It does
indicate that the book contains nothing contrary to Catholic faith or
morals.

TABLE OF CONTENTS

PART FOUR: A REVOLUTION OF LOVE

PHOTOGRAPHS

After PART TWO

A WORD OF RECOMMENDATION
by Stephen Cardinal Kim

These words were written by Cardinal Kim, Archbishop of Seoul, in September 1993, just prior to Eileen's third visit to Korea, as a foreword to the Korean translation of the book Eileen George: Beacon of God's Love: Her Teaching.

I would like to simply introduce Mrs. Eileen George to you... This woman loves God the Father very, very much and wishes to share with people all over the world the knowledge of God's love.

Eileen George has been to our country twice, and now it makes me happy to think she will visit us a third time.

In 1989 Eileen shared her teaching with priests, brothers and sisters numbering 80,000. From her whole heart and soul she gave to many God the Father's love, peace and joy. In seeing Eileen George we see what can happen to us ordinary people, too. We should feel moved to rise above ourselves to wholehearted self-giving.

At this time it is my hopeful wish for all Korean Christians, that, as we gladly meet and receive Eileen's spiritual teaching, we will allow that teaching to make a big change in our Faith-life.

FOREWORD

Eileen George's Conversations in Heaven II is the second in a series of books containing Eileen George's conversations with Jesus and the Father. The first volume related those conversations which occurred in 1982. They prepared Eileen for her public mission. This second volume relates her conversations during the year 1983 while her mission was underway and gathering momentum.

This series was preceded by the publication of *Eileen George: Beacon of God's Love: Her Teaching.* This book "was published in 1990 eight years after Eileen's public ministry began. It presents her public teaching given in parish renewals, conferences, retreats, and in her publicly distributed meditative tapes. It also relates facts about her life, her mission and her credibility. And it shows how her mission is being accomplished in the power of the Spirit and in accord with the Scriptures and the teaching of the Church" (Introduction to *Conversations in Heaven,* page 7).

Conversations in Heaven, on the other hand, "records dialogues between Eileen, Jesus and the Father . . . Prophecy is proven by the occurrence of the foretold event. In this book we see foretold Eileen's far reaching mission, which has since taken place . . . So the Father's predictions and instructions regarding Eileen's mission made in 1982 and related in this book have been fulfilled in the intervening ten years . . .

"Eileen's hearers and readers recognize that she speaks from experience about the kingdom and about the persons of the Trinity. They wish to know more of her actual experiences — to go 'behind the scenes.' *Conversations in Heaven* takes them behind the scenes . . ." *(Conversations in Heaven,* pages 7-9)

In taking the readers "behind the scenes," we come upon features of Heaven which raise questions and doubts. In *Conversations in Heaven,* those doubts were addressed by a number of self-consistent considerations, making more plausible what Eileen relates. To quote from that book: " 'Eye has not seen nor ear heard what God has prepared for those who love Him.'

"Nevertheless it is not inconceivable that all grades of beings made by the Father in His Son and through the Holy Spirit, are present in Heaven. We expect a new earth and new heavens, and they may contain plants and animals, brooks, fields and mountains. 'Then I saw a new heaven and a new earth; the first heavens and the first earth had disappeared now, and there was no longer any sea' (Rev 21:1). 'What we are waiting for, relying on his promises, is the new heavens and the new earth, where uprightness will be at home' (2 Peter 3:13). 'For we are well aware that when the tent that houses us on earth is folded up, there is a house for us from God, not made by human hands but everlasting, in the heavens' (2 Cor 5:1)" (the Introduction to *Conversations in Heaven,* pages 11-12).

Two more particulars will be of help in reading the dialogues that follow. These dialogues were recorded by Eileen's spiritual director during her thanksgiving after Mass said privately. Where Eileen meditatively repeats the words of the Father or Jesus, these words are set in bold type, as also are those words repeated by Eileen at the request of the Father or Jesus.

During her thanksgiving, Eileen is unaware of her surroundings and of being taped. These tapes contain revelations of Eileen's special relations with the Father, Jesus and the Spirit, and of her special prerogatives in view of her mission. They also indicate something of her sufferings on behalf of souls, which are part of this record now published for the welfare of souls and of the Church by her spiritual director.

Then there is the name "Butchie." The Introduction to the first volume of this series relates that "It was necessary to make a decision about Eileen's manner of addressing Jesus as 'Butchie.' Reluctantly the editor has replaced this familiar term of address. To understand it one needs to know that before the age of three the Father took Eileen in hand by giving her as a companion, playmate and teacher a child about two or three years older than herself, who grew up with her. This companion said to her, 'Call me Butchie, and I'll call you Slug.' A few years later Eileen realized that Butchie was Jesus. From then on she reverenced Him as the Son of God, but she continued to call Him 'Butchie.'

"God's desire to be with us on familiar terms led the Son of God to the womb of the Virgin, to the Cross, and to the Host where He becomes our food. After that, is it surprising that to this dear child of His, He is 'Butchie?' "

In this book I am not replacing the name by which Eileen addresses Jesus. I realize that the name 'Jesus' contains power, sweetness and salvation. That Eileen calls Him 'Butchie' is one of the inimitable things in their relationship.

PART ONE: "THIS DANGEROUS FREE WILL"

1. "THIS WILL BE OUR BEST YEAR"
January 2, 1983

I don't really want to talk, Butchie. I just want to sit here with You and be quiet..... I wasn't thinking of much, so how can I tell You?..... I was just wondering. I love You so much. Do I love You as a person I love, or do I love You as the Son of the Father? I'm trying to find out which makes the deeper impression upon my soul..... I haven't reached a conclusion. I love You when I'm with You as a person that I can feel and touch and love. When I'm not with You in this way, I feel You within me. When You make Yourself visible, I don't love You more, I love You the same. But I know You are the Father's Son. I was wondering in which way I love You the most..... Am I confusing You? I don't mean to..... Of course I love You when You make Yourself visible to me. But I love You when You are inside of me. I love You always.....

I guess I'm peaceful. Does it show?..... Thank You..... Why are You asking me that? What would You ask Him for?..... Really? **That I be with You always and forever and get out of this world.** But I have work to do, and I'm not ready. Don't You start pushing it. I have a lot of things I have to fix in my life..... Well, thank You. I'm glad You accept me this way, but I still have a lot of things I have to do. I want the Father to be proud of me. But if He called me I certainly wouldn't hesitate. But don't You start pushing it. Let me look better for Him..... That's for You. But I want to look perfect for the Father..... Oh, You say that, but I know what's wrong with me in different areas, Butchie..... No, it's nice of You to say it, but I have a lot of polishing to do, and I need the time..... Aw, You are so silly..... I know You do, and I love You too, but I want to be perfect for the Father.....

I never get so involved with the ministry. Not to the point of slighting You. Do I? How could I forget You, even for a moment..... But I ask You to stand beside me. I know You are there. I see You walking up and down the aisle like a big shot. So You are with me, right?

Butchie, this will be our best year. I'll try to be so good for You and for the Father, and Your Spirit will help me. He promised when I was saying my novena *[to Him].....* Listen You, You know I didn't say it today. Yesterday..... I don't call that loving me, You're always trying to trip me..... (laughs) Watch and see if You are on Your own toes. I'll worry about my toes.....

Well, You can come and see me anytime You wish. I do want to be here forever, but I have things to do for the Father..... Are You really glad that I say that?..... Yes, it's beautiful here. I would never want to go back. I wish I could stay. But I have to make myself better for the Father and I have to bring more people to Him..... Thank You. I know You understand.....

I love You, too..... Thank You. I'm glad You are proud of me. But we're going to be better for the Father. You're going to help me, Butchie, right? And the Spirit will help me, and Mary will help me..... Yes, I call upon Michael. I'm keeping him closer than ever, because of the spirits..... I don't want to talk about them. You know I call upon Michael, and when I sleep I ask him to watch over me.....

You'll never lose me..... Butch, You sound like a jealous old husband..... That was Your purpose and now it is mine, to let them know the Father.....

No, Father. Butchie said it was His purpose to reveal the Father. It's my purpose to help Butchie reveal You, right, my Father?..... (laughs) Yes, He is giving me a hard time. He wants me to stay here forever and ever. I told Him I have to become a better person. I have a lot of corners to polish. (laughs) He says He likes me the way I am. But I want to be better, Father. I want You to be proud of me, and I want to bring many people to know You, my Father. Butchie is just teasing. He's going to help me along with the Spirit.....

Whatever You want me to talk about..... You act like You're excited about these talks, my Father..... I don't know. I think two things, Father. When I go out and eager faces are lifted towards me, like they are hungry for the word, I think that's one of the greatest moments. I think the second is the priests at Benediction looking up and admiring Jesus in reverence and love. I think those are the highlights..... Thank you, Father. I'd be happy about that. I'd love to have many more priests come.....

Well, I think the healings are wonderful. But I don't think they are the highlight..... They could be a climax. The people are seeking them from Jesus and the Father out of love, so He gives them a little bit of frosting on the cake. They are physical, but for me, it's the spiritual healings *[that are best]*, Father, especially a healing with their God..... Thank You, Father.

Yes, I do feel the Spirit. He's bringing me peace, my Father. I feel free and peaceful and very much in love with the Trinity, Father..... Yes, I know You have chosen me. I don't deserve it, and I don't know why, but I accept it, and I'll do anything You ask, my Father..... Are You really proud of that? I don't want to hurt anyone's feelings, but I want to stand firm. Father X says I emphasize "Catholic" too much. Do You agree with him, my Father?..... I didn't think You would. I didn't say anything to him and I didn't tell anybody what he said. But I told him I wouldn't be a jelly fish. I would stand firm. That's what it's all about.....

Do You think that I hurt anyone, Father? I try to be as gentle as the Spirit leads me to be..... **I must stand firm on Catholic doctrine and tradition or else my faith will be in danger.....** Father, what about those who are coming who are not Christian or are Christian but not Catholic? I don't want to hurt them..... **They will** realize where I am coming from, and they will want to come from there. It will be their starting point. They will say she does not waver. She is strong in her faith. She speaks but truth. I thank You, Father.....

With my whole heart and soul. I've never wavered but I've grown deeper and deeper in love with You, my Father. How could I not love You? I love everything about You. I love Your face and Your hair, the softness and depth in Your eyes, Your warmth. I feel safe with You, Father. Protected and loved. I never question Your love. That means so much, never having to question it. I know it's there all the time, always, Father.....

"You will go into the world as a new dawn and many will come back to the fold. The priests of the high altars will return, for you will put them to shame. You will draw the sisters back to their faith, to their calling, for they will realize that they are the brides of Christ and that they have drifted. Then My children will hunger and thirst for the same God that you speak of, that you radiate. Yes, Eileen, your mission will be great and you will grow deeper in love with your Father, and you will isolate yourself when your work is done. You will go into the desert and be alone with Him Who loves you and teaches you."

INTERVIEW

Butchie can't wait until He gets you there?

I was tempted today.

He was tempting you?

He certainly was. But there's work to be done. I have a lot of faults. I want to please the Father and clean off these edges. And I'd like to bring more people to Him.

They are going to help you to come closer to Them?

Yes.

Was Butchie afraid you would get involved with ministry?

Yes, He was. He said, "You know all these people are demanding your attention more and more, Eileen. I know you don't forget Me, but I get jealous. I believe that you gave them what you can and you should leave it at that." I do think I give them the best I can. It may not be the best for them, but it's the best I can do. They should accept it. They go downstairs *[after the monthly service]* for a cup of coffee and they are standing there like this, waiting to grab me. So I run down the back stairs. And the next thing I know, they say, "There she is." And I'm trying to get to my daughter and Peter or to somebody who really needs me, like that little boy. They are pulling me and the cameras are flashing.

So what did the Father think?

I had thought of going home by another door. The Father said, "No, I don't want them to think you think you are high and mighty. I want them to know that you walk amongst them, that you are one of them." He wants them to know that I love them and that I'm walking with them.

Butchie said He was jealous?

Oh, the trailer, the telephone . . .

So what did He suggest?

"Come and stay at the Castle." I'm trying to talk to Him and He kisses me.

2. "I TURN TO THEM FOR COMFORT AND THEY COMFORT ME NOT"
January 5, 1983

[Eileen has spoken to a religious Superior.]

For sure I am downhearted over it, Butchie..... I don't know what I can do besides pray. I feel it because of the Father. This is only one community. Imagine how many more are hurting Him. I just want to comfort Him, and to love Him and to be lost in Him..... No, it breaks my heart to think how much sorrow He feels because of these people. They are hurting Him and maybe they are not even aware of it. If they are, why don't they stop? I don't see why the Father has to go through all this, Butchie.....

It seems like there's no end. I would just like to hide some place and be with the Father forever. Cut free from everybody. Just spend my time loving Him and comforting Him. It blows my mind that they would do this..... No, I don't think it's old Church [keeping the rules]. Do You?.....

I don't know what we can do about it. I don't want the Father to hurt so much. If they only realized how much they are hurting Him..... **I turn to them for comfort, and they comfort me not. Not alone and not enough that they crucified My Son, but they do it to Me over and over again. If I could bleed the blood of humans, it would have been over a long time ago, but the infinite blood of God spills forever. If My tears could run out, they would be gone a long time ago. But the infinite God can cry forever.....**

I don't like that, Butchie. I don't like that at all..... You know what I wish? That I could go away to the top of a mountain and stay there forever with the Father..... Of course You could come. We could comfort Him together. We would not show Him any sadness, just love. I hurt more for Him, Butchie, because nothing can be kept from Him. If I could hide it I would, so as not to bring

Him discomfort or hurt.....

Yes, I guess that's why He's calling me to this mission. I don't understand it fully, but I'm willing *[to accept it]*..... Yes, I am down about it. I hurt awful for the Father. I knew what was going on, but to hear him *[the Superior]* and to know that he knows it and does nothing about it, it wounds me deeply..... **It wounds the Father twice as much.....** I know. We'll do it together, You and I.....

For sure I'll hold Your hand and we will love Him and comfort Him..... I don't want to think about that. I don't want to wipe His tears, because I don't want to see Him cry. I can't bear to see Him cry..... I know. But they have such a golden opportunity to do so *[to comfort the Father]*, and yet they don't. I don't want to judge them. But what is white is white and what is black is black. If their hearts are hardened, then there's a lot of evil there, Butch. And if their hearts are not hardened, they know it's wrong. So either way, it's bad! I can't see how they love the Father. I don't think they know Him, else they wouldn't do this.....

Sure I'm touched deeply. I'm hurting for the Father, aren't You?..... Poor Butchie, You are so good, You must hurt for Him more than I do..... Well, I'm glad You rejoice in my sadness, but it doesn't make me feel much better..... You know I love the Father. I never want to bring Him sadness..... Just listening to him *[the Superior]* talk about everything that is going on and knowing it, I resolved more than ever to comfort the Father.....

Look at Him! He looks lonely..... Will He, Butchie? Butchie says the moment You see me You will rejoice, my Father. I feel so bad about everything they do to You, Father..... I know I do many things, but I feel so sad today about everything that's going on. I just wish they knew You better, Father. And then knowing You they would only want to love You. I don't see how it could be possible for them to be there and not know You or love You. I just can't grasp it, my Father..... Yes, I know I lose my temper at times, but I know You are there. I'm aware of Your presence, even if You are not visible to me at times, my Father.....

I can't understand their cutting themselves free and hurting You continually..... Then why are they there?..... But it's not a job. It's a calling, my Father, it's a vocation, right?..... I know. I do pray. How can I not feel sad when I love You so much? I ache for You, my Father.....

I know You are big. But I still ache for You. I know You are sensitive, far more than we..... Father, I want to love You more than anybody in the whole world, and I will do anything I can to help them. Let them experience Your love, my Father. Then they'll be good..... But if they experience Your love, they won't be naughty any more. They could never hurt you, at least not intentionally.....

If they truly believed You were everywhere, they wouldn't be doing these things. Make them aware of that, Father. Help them. You can do anything, Father. I know You won't force the will, but couldn't You just blow them away with grace, Father? Touch them deeply, by a word or something, Father..... Of course I feel for them. I know You love them and want them to be good. So that's why I hurt so much..... Well, I hurt for him, too *[the Superior]*. I know it will kill him *[to be removed from office]*, my Father..... Can't You give him perseverance *[in his good resolutions]*?..... Well, make him ask for it. You can do anything, Father. Touch him by grace to ask for perseverance.....

3. THE HOLY YEAR AND SANCTITY
January 30, 1983

I'm on my way to the monastery to see my spiritual director. I'll try to record my conversation with the Father.

My Father, I find it very difficult to leave the house on Sunday. I search my soul over and over. Is it important that I leave my house on Sunday? Will You please answer me, my Father, and I will repeat so that I can go over this tape again to satisfy my mind, my body and my soul that I am doing the right thing.

Eileen, it is very important that you get away from the noise and the frustration at least once a week. You need this time in order to draw deeper and deeper into the Sacred Heart of My Son and into the Father's arms. For in these quiet moments you hear the wisdom of the Father. Eileen, just like a furnace has to be fed fuel, whether it be oil, wood or gas, to keep the house warm, you have to be fed the word of the Father and there is no better time than in the silence and solitude of the monastery.

I understand, my Father. Look at that beautiful pigeon sitting on that housetop. He looks so alone, and yet he seems to be observing the whole world.

Yes, Child, that is how you are at the monastery. You begin to observe and see exactly what the Father expects of you. You are observing everyone and everything, yet you are alone in My Son's Sacred Heart. And here is where you find My wisdom, My knowledge and My understanding.

Yes, I understand that, Father. I must walk alone in spirit, and here is where I will have time to collect my thoughts through the light of the Holy Spirit. Here is where I will be nourished and fed the word of my Father. And I'll be able to give it to our people. I do miss these quiet moments *[which she had in her house before it burned down in September.]* I know I should be making so many tapes, and I'm longing to be in that house [the new house being built] and get back to a normal, happy life, a life of silence and solitude, where I can make more tapes for You, my Father. I'm so afraid I won't be saying or giving the messages that You want, Father, because of all the noise and frustration. Father, please help me to finish my house soon. I know we can do it, Father, and I know You want me there as soon as possible.

I love You, Father. I'm soaking in all the beauty of Your world. Its majesty, the mountains, the hills. Everything is so beautiful, Father. And I feel so rich in Your love. I wish just You and I could be together always..... We will?! Will it be very soon?..... No, I'm not trying to twist Your arm..... Thank You, Father.

Eileen, at this moment you see all the peace around you. And I want so much for this peace to last upon earth. But this year of all years, the devil will be seeking souls to devour.

But, Father, isn't he always seeking souls to devour?

Yes, Child, but this will be a year in which he will reach out to more souls to try to snatch them away from the light of the Spirit. Pray for My people, Eileen.

I will, my Father, I certainly will.

You know, Eileen, this year will be declared the Holy Year. There is a reason for this.

Is the reason because the Vatican is in financial trouble?

Yes, Eileen, this brought it about. But I have a reason for the declaration of this Holy Year, because this is the year the devil is out to devour My people. The blessings of this Holy Year will more than balance the work of Capi, Eileen. I will draw good from it.

You mean there will be a Holy Year because the Vatican is in financial trouble and You will draw good from it? I understand the balance, and I think it's super.

But the devil is having a fit, Child, because of this Holy Year. He knows that I am interfering with him, and that I will center

the light of the Holy Spirit on My people.

I think that's beautiful, Father. I thank You for letting me in on Your secrets. I will pray and I will tell my director why You are bringing the Holy Year about at this time. Thank You, Father..... You mean that while the devil has his workers out trying to gain more people for his kingdom, this Holy Year, You will send Michael and Raphael, the angels and archangels to walk more closely to God's people to protect them and bring blessings upon them?

Yes, my Child, this is it. Eileen, this is going to be a bad year for the Church. Even the rules which the Holy Father has just made *[the new Code of Canon Law]*, God's priests are trying to separate themselves from them and interpret them in their own way. You must pray for them, Eileen, that they may have the wisdom of their God. Eileen, for seven years or more, according to your time, the Holy Father has been disobeyed. This year is going to be no different. They are going to defy him, and turn against him. You must pray for him, Eileen. He is a very holy man and pleasing to the Father. All he wants is to glorify his God and be obedient to the Commandments of God. Eileen, pray for him. Watch over him by prayer. He needs prayers. Resort to the power of prayer, Child.

You see, Child, when one tries to walk in the light of the Holy Spirit and to live in the true Church in its doctrine, tradition and discipline one is going to be rejected. Eileen, there is a great work cut out for you. But by the grace of the Father, in close union with the Son, and walking in the light of the Spirit, you can do it. Do not be offended or feel rejected because they reject you, as long as the Father accepts you. You are walking in His righteousness and love. I know at times it will be difficult and you will hurt. But remember, Eileen, you are doing My will and I am always with you.

Eileen, do you feel the peace as you enter this monastery road? These monks will have a lot to give an account to the Father for. I put them in a little paradise where they can worship their God, enjoy the beauty that surrounds them, where they can meditate and draw closer to My Son. Yes, they will have to give an account of the blessings I have given to them. Much has been given to them, and much will be asked of them. Eileen, they hold sainthood at their finger tips. Pray for them, Child. Pray for them.

4. FREE WILL CAN BRING THE SOUL TO HELL
January 30, 1983

We haven't walked this way for quite a long time, Butchie. It's my favorite path..... I think every path is beautiful. But I like this path the best..... I don't know why. It's our secret place. It's ours, it belongs to us. I'm delighted with every turn. Everything is so beautiful. I feel myself swelling, as if I could not take any more of its beauty.....

When I look at You I feel Your love. I feel as though Your love is sinking into the depths of my soul..... When I say my soul, I don't quite understand what part, but the depths. It touches a deep, deep part of me. That's how I feel. I don't know if I can explain it well enough, Butchie. But that's what Your love does, it touches the depth of my soul.....

I can't figure out the soul..... At this moment I'm seeing something violet, yet white, something white but violet, something beautiful, unique. I know You touch the depths of it with Your love, with just Your glance. It's like an ocean, like space. You know, Butchie, what I'm trying to say.....

It has a glow. It belongs to the Father, yet it's mine. I'm aware of it now, Butchie, more than ever before. My soul! My foot, my hand, my body — but my soul! There's a beginning and end to my foot, my hand, my body, but there's no beginning or end to my soul..... No, I'm not uncomfortable with it. I feel great peace with it. But I can't quite understand what You are trying to tell me.....

Yes, I feel no end to it. It's there. It's like white haze, spaceless, bottomless. I know You've touched my soul..... No, I don't feel it round or square or oblong. I can't explain it. Butchie, You know what I mean. You are making me aware of it. I can't quite grasp it all. Yet I'm aware of my soul at this moment, Butchie.

I've never been aware of my soul like this before. My soul. My soul. It rings like bells in the air. It's beautiful and sweet. I have a soul. My Father gave it to me. With the soul I can get to Heaven. But not all souls get here, Butchie. Why don't they all get here then?..... **They reject grace and in rejecting grace they sin. But it's not the poor soul's fault.....** I remember that rabbit. It screamed awful, Butchie. It pains me to think about it..... I remember the dogs. The stray dogs caught it and it screamed. My Father said this is how the soul screams in the hands of the devil *[when he takes it to Hell]*. We have an obligation to our soul. What a terrible thing to have your soul go to Hell when it cries for God!.....

I think it's a tremendous thing You are telling me. Yet it's frightening me..... No, I know You don't mean to frighten me. What a terrible responsibility we have towards the soul. It wants God. It is up to us by acceptance of grace to bring our soul to God..... I've never felt bad for a soul before. I did for a person. There's something deeper within that person. A soul that cries for God. A person with their free will can keep that soul from God. Butchie, this is frightening.....

I do want to be the best person ever this Lent. And now even more strongly. Butchie, I have a tremendous obligation to my soul. More than I could ever grasp before. Our own free will can deprive our soul. It's terrible. It's awful, Butchie..... You feel terrible for the person, but it's even worse for the soul. I knew that a person who sins sends himself to Hell, but it never dawned on me that the soul falling into Hell screams for God, and the person is taking it down. How terrible!

Father, it's the teaching Butchie's given me about the soul. I know what He said is true. But as humans we don't understand this. This is a tremendous revelation and only by the awareness of the Spirit can I grasp it..... For sure, my Father. I always thought of the person going to Hell. I know that the person has a soul, and that Jesus died for the person. But it never dawned on me that the person is pulling to Hell a soul that's crying for God. The free will can do this..... That's what I meant, Father, we have a tremendous responsibility for our soul..... Yes, I know it's the Spirit that's enlightening me, Father, and I thank You..... It's frightening. I know You don't want to frighten me. I was telling Butchie that when He looked at me, I felt His eyes piercing my soul. Then all of a sudden I became aware of my soul. It was like a space but not a space, a bottomless pit, but not a frightening one. Like purplish white, hazy and beautiful. Without sides, top, bottom. My soul. My soul meant so much when Butchie looked at me revealing it.....

For sure I can think about it. It would be a meditation in itself. But I don't think I could ever reach deeper knowledge of it than You gave me through the Spirit..... Really? **A resolution for Lent.** I usually try not to make them, my Father. But I do want to be the best person ever this Lent. And the Spirit is helping me through the revelation about the soul, about my soul. I know everything is given to me by You, Father. The soul! A soul that wants to get back to God forever! It's blowing my mind, Father..... 'Course I see how You love me, Father. Maybe not as I should, but according to the light You give me. You know how dopey I am..... This means so much to me. I have a soul!

I always knew I had a soul. But it means so much to me: a soul that wants to get back to my Father. I musn't ever sin or put blockages in its way. The soul wants to be free and sail straight towards my Father..... Yes, Father. Through Your love and goodness I understand. What can I do without the Holy Spirit? I love the Spirit so much, Father. He gives me light to understand everything You want me to know..... **It's only the beginning of the teaching You'll give me for Lent. These revelations will be very important. Eileen, you must write them down.** Father, I will. I promise..... I'm sure they know they have a soul, but like myself, I think we've never thought about it. We know it, but never got into what our free will does to the soul.....

What about the animals? You've shown me animals here in the Castle They haven't got a soul like mine, Father, but they will be enjoying Heaven..... **They'll be existing with love, without pain. With my soul, I'll be enjoying Heaven to the fullest.** Yes, it makes me special. I feel very special. You could have made me a skunk, or a dog, or a cat. I feel very special, Father. Eileen has a soul. It's blowing my mind. It's sinking deeper, Father.....

Again You say You'll give me many revelations in the holy season of Lent..... I really hope You do give me many revelations during Lent, Father, as the weeks go by. I know it's the beginning of something great..... **These must never pass. You must write them down.** I will, Father. I'm excited about it.

But what more can You tell me about the soul? Father, I want to know so many things, but only as You unfold them to me, Father. You teach me such wonderful things..... Sure, I'm Your little girl. And they are not stories, they are true.....

I am deeply touched, Father. It's because You take time out to talk to me, Father. It's because You care. You want me to know things..... How can I help but cry? I know You love me. You reveal so many secrets to me. I know what I'm made of. I know how dumb I can be.....

This will be the best Lent ever. I will try so hard to please You, my Father. I want to be the best person ever..... You want me to make a tape about the soul? What will I call the tape?..... **"The reformation of the soul." And it must not be made known now.....** Until when, my Father?..... **Give it to my director and You will inspire him.** Whatever You say, my Father..... I love You with my whole heart, my whole mind, my body and truly with my soul. Mine, given to me by my Father. Nobody can take my soul from me. But my free will can destroy it for all eternity..... I know Your justice..... I love You forever.

INTERVIEW

Do you want to tell me what the Father told you about the soul?

I don't know where to begin. We hear many times that we have a body and soul. But now I know it in my depths. I, Eileen, have a soul. It's blowing my mind. You could call it a spirit. As He revealed it, it has no size, no form nor shape. He was telling me that the soul will live forever, and where I send it is my responsibility according to my free will. It is such a tremendous responsibility. God gave us a soul, and the soul wants to go back to God. With our free will we can bring the soul to Hell. We can put it there while it is screeching for God. What a terrible thing! Do you understand what I am telling you?

Yes. That is the pain of loss. The pain of loss wouldn't be so terrible if the soul didn't want God so much.

It's a terrible thing. We say that we are responsible for ourself. We should really say we are responsible for the future of our soul: Heaven or Hell. God loved me enough to give me a soul so that it could go back to Him. But we are pulling it in a different direction. When Capi gets a soul, the soul is screaming because it wants God, and we put it into the eternal fires. It almost makes me sick. My Father compared it with a rabbit. You remember once I told you that I saw stray dogs running and cornering a rabbit in my neighbor's fence. That rabbit screamed because the dogs got it. My Father said that's how the soul screams when the devil gets it. He said this coming Lent He is going to give me many revelations. He wants me to do a tape on the soul and give it to you. It is not to be made public till I'm not around.

After you go to the Castle it can be published?

Yes. He said I must write all the revelations down that He will give me this Lent. And if I have the time, put them on tape. It has more meaning when put on tape.

About the soul, it is blowing my mind. It began when Butchie and I were walking. He looked at me with His love. I knew at that moment He had touched the depth of my soul. It was like a light turned on. I knew His love had touched my soul. What is a soul? I saw purple and white, haziness, lightness and no shape. Can you understand what I'm telling you?

Yes, it is not material, so it has no shape.

I knew His love touched the depth of my soul. And all of a sudden I saw the soul. I knew it was by the light of the Spirit. I also knew the importance of the salvation of the soul. I always knew we had a body and a soul. But this time I knew it in a different way. I have a soul, what a tremendous gift! I said, "Father, You showed me animals in Heaven and in my Castle. They don't have a soul, like I do." He said, Eileen, "I put them there for your enjoyment. You are the one I'm out to please and to give My kingdom to, because you have a soul given by the Father." The animals will not enjoy Heaven as I enjoy Heaven. They were put there for my good, because I love them and I am the one who has a soul. He told me to think about it in the coming week.

PART TWO: THE PRICE

5. ALL THAT PAIN FOR ONE PERSON
February 6, 1983

Everything that comes from the Father is good. So how can I make the soul beautiful?..... Yes, I see..... Back up now. **Take an apple from the tree. It is dull. The more I polish it the more beautiful it becomes, and the more appetizing. Then you eat it. The Father gave the soul and it is beautiful.** He sends streams of graces by which the virtues can be practised which polish the soul and make it more pleasing to the Father. Humility, obedience, patience. He gives me the polish I need: the graces. And the soul becomes shiny and more beautiful. Sin is abusive and cruel treatment of the soul. I understand it now.....

Well, the Father said when we sin or are unkind and don't practise the virtues, we are abusing the soul, we're disfiguring our soul. How can we disfigure the soul by sin?..... Almost like cruel and abusive treatment..... **Exactly.** That gives me the creeps. I don't like that stuff..... **It's reality.** What's reality got to do with the soul?..... **It's spiritual. I can't exist without it.** The Father says I'm not capable of one action without it. Not one good action..... Sometimes my Father's talks are very deep, Butchie..... But You began this talk Yourself, and the Father finished it..... No, I don't mind if He sets my head spinning, so long as I have the grace to stop it and grasp what He's trying to tell me.....

Do You feel the same way the Father does, Butchie, when a soul goes to Hell?..... **You died for that soul.....** I think I understand..... **You died especially for that soul, and its free will caused it to go to Hell.** But You died for all of us, Butchie. How can You single out one soul from the rest of us..... **You died to save that soul.** For every individual soul?..... I know that. But I have never singled out one like that before, Butch..... That's awfully hard for me to understand. You better send that Spirit to me..... **You died** for all of us, and yet, You died for that one soul. And the person that condemned that soul to Hell with his free will caused You to go through that suffering. That's awfully hard for me to understand..... Yes, I know You died for all of us. I understand that, and I heard that if I were the only one on earth, You would die for me..... But You mean for that one person, all that suffering was in vain..... I wouldn't want to be that person, then.....

Well, sure, it scares me to death, Butchie, I'm frightened..... No, to see You there upon the cross, and to realize that it was just me who caused it..... I know You don't mean to frighten us. You just want to alert us and put us on the path to salvation..... Butchie, now listen here, if I told somebody that, they'd be scared out of their wits..... **Rightfully so. They should be?.....** Now You sound like the Father in the Old Testament..... Sometimes I don't know what reality is.

I would never want to be the cause of Your suffering. I have to get that teaching straight, Butchie. You died for every one of us, and yet, for one. So if I cause, God forbid, my soul to go to Hell by continually sinning and not asking for the Father's forgiveness and it was deliberate and sent my soul to Hell, for that one, for me, all those pains You suffered would be useless. But what about the rest of the people? How can You separate me from the rest of the people like that?..... Well, I guess I know You're God, for sure, but that's awful deep, Butchie. You better send the Spirit. That's hard for me to understand.....

You may not want to stump me, but You have..... You died for all, but for one. Then I have a terrible responsibility, to make sure that for this one, Eileen, You didn't suffer and die in vain because I'm condemning my soul to Hell. That's scary. I hope nobody ever does that, Butchie.....

For sure I'll pray. I'll do anything You want. I don't want one of these people to make their soul go to Hell, and to have You go through all that pain for that one person in vain..... For all and yet for one. That's awful deep, Butchie..... Of course I believe everything You tell me. But don't forget my mind isn't like Yours, Butch.....

You'll have to help me more with that, it's awful hard. I see and yet I can't see. I think I understand, and yet I waiver..... It is hard for me to grasp. I know You died for all of us, and yet for each individual soul..... I just can't grasp how if one allows him or herself to go to Hell Your suffering is in vain, although You suffered for all of us.

Your suffering was for a personal relationship with every one of us, just with me, just with her, just with him. You did it on a personal basis..... Well, if they're all this deep, I'll have a headache all the time. You forget who You're dealing with, Butchie. You must remember it's me..... Yes, I remember the Spirit.....

I love Your teachings and I love the Father's teachings, but I love to be here and to be quiet and to enjoy everything..... Nope, I'm not trying to distract You..... Well, I was never that much of a scholar. I could care less..... **Not for myself** *[these teachings].* How will I know what they will do with it?..... Well, I'll trust You.....

I like to know things, but I like to be able to grasp them, Butchie. I can't grasp everything..... For sure I'm depending on the Spirit..... I'm trying to go back to what You said. You died for all of us, and yet on an individual basis. If a person commits a mortal sin and his soul goes to Hell, that person condemned his soul to Hell. Then for that one person, You went through all this suffering, and he is accountable..... Now I understand. For sure it's the work of the Spirit. For all, and yet for each one of us. We have the responsibility of cooperating with grace because of Your suffering for us on the cross..... So the mortal sin is bad enough, but causing the Savior to die upon the cross and throwing all His graces away is worse.

Wow! I don't think I ever looked at it that way, Butchie. How can You blame us for something we don't know?..... But I think You're blaming..... Well, I don't know too much about Revelation. I don't think I could ever put that across. Look how hard a time I had trying to grasp it. Good thing the Spirit stands close by..... Of course I love the Spirit. You've seen what I am without Him — nothing..... Yes, every day. Butchie. I know how much I need Him..... I am so dopey and dumb without Him, I need Him in everything I do.....

Father, I always looked at Lent as a joyful season. I'm so thrilled to do something for Butchie. He's done so much for me..... I know it's a time of penance, but if you love then that penance is a joy..... Butchie, then You agree with me, right?.....

(laughs) Father, He agrees with me because I said Lent was a joyful season..... I don't know how I came to it. Because I love Butchie and I love the Father and the Spirit, and if You're giving me this extra season to do something to make Them understand how much I love Them, then I feel joyful.....

(laughs) It's not a season of ashes and rags..... Well, You said to use it for loving.....

He was giving me a teaching, my Father, I found it so hard to understand..... Yes, I called upon the Spirit. I just couldn't separate things..... (laughs) Oh Butchie, I think You're a very good teacher. It's me..... Yes, Father, I never quite understood it that way. I understood He died for every one of us upon the cross, and yet, I couldn't understand how if He died for all of us how He could separate Himself in the suffering department and a person that willfully threw himself and his soul into Hell and abused Jesus' suffering, because of that person His suffering was in vain.

If He died for all of us, how could it be in vain for that one person? Butchie said he neglected grace. So the person abused the Savior and His grace, and that sin is far greater, right, Father?.....

Who did You tell that to?..... **Thomasino.....** (laughs) Well, if they're all like this, I think You better quit while you've got a head start.....

For sure I trust in the Spirit..... Father, whenever I say I trust in Him and I love Him, the glow is brighter than ever, and it seems to pulsate even more..... Is that His way of saying He loves me?..... And I feel His love. I feel it in His wisdom, in His light. I feel it when He possesses my very being, all warm and aglow..... A third person..... I know it's true, because I experience Him, my Father..... I feel Him wedded to my soul and to my mind, to my heart.....

He's part of me, because I can't function without Him, Father. Almost like Mary couldn't function as Jesus' Mother without Him. In a different way, and yet, almost the same. And my love grows deeper for Him, Father..... **It will deepen more this Lent.** That fills me full of joy, Father. A deep, deep peace, because I depend on Him so much. I know what I'm capable of doing and understanding.....

I truly love You, Holy Spirit, and I truly need You. You see what I'm capable of doing without You. I respond to Your love. I feel Your light and Your wisdom and Your knowledge, and I know these are acts of love of me. It's hard, in my humanness, to understand You, and yet, I love You, and I can't quite understand my love for You. I know You're alive. I sense You in me and around me. And this day I know more than ever how much I need You. At this moment I know You're pleased with me, and I'm delighted.....

Yes, Father. If I learn nothing more this day, I have learned a mountain full, enough to fill its space.

INTERVIEW

You were talking to Butchie about how it amazes you that everything comes from the Father, and the Father makes everything good, but you can make the soul beautiful. And He explained how you do that by the example of polishing an apple?

He did.

And you asked Him if He felt the same way the Father does when a soul goes to Hell?

Yes. It's so hard to grasp what He was telling me. He died on the cross, Father, for everybody, and yet, He died for me alone, for you alone. Now, if I, God forbid, lead a sinful life and commit mortal sins and cast myself and my soul into Hell, then all that suffering on the cross I cause to be in vain because I abused it and all His graces. **So, for this one individual, He said, Eileen, I died in vain for you. I died to give you the graces and you rejected them.**

So it must have caused Him suffering on the cross to see that soul. Did He say anything about that? He saw the individual soul rejecting the grace that He was suffering to give him?

And plunging himself into Hell.

He saw that on the cross, and that made Him suffer more because He was in pain for that person?

But He, as God, could separate this. He died for all. Yes, but He could see each one individually as if that one was the only soul in the world. Isn't it awful — how He must have suffered. And it wasn't just a physical suffering, all that mental anguish. **"I'm going through all this, and you're not. The graces, you're not using them, you're rejecting them. So, for you, I suffer for nothing."**

And it was on the cross He experienced that?

He saw it all. How terrible, huh?

And then you said something about, it sounds like the Father in the Old Testament, because you were scared.

Yes.

And He said He just wanted to alert us to understand what mortal sin is?

Yes, our responsibility.

So why did it sound like the Old Testament? Because it scared you?

Yes, for sure. Telling me the great responsibility we have, casting the soul into Hell. And then He said, "Well, that's reality, and I want you to know reality." It's hard to understand. He died for all and some respond, so it's not in vain for them. Then how could it be in vain? For the individual that rejects the grace, for that individual it is in vain. See how important it is for one soul not to be lost. So it's very important that I try to save souls by preaching and by everything.

And then you said mortal sin is bad enough, but it's worse in causing the Savior to die on the cross.

And in vain, for that one person. Rejecting grace is terrible.

And you said, "How can You blame us for what we don't know?" What did He say about that?

"You have a responsibility in life to go into it."

And He said that in Revelation He explained that?

Yes. He said we should look more into the teachings. And He said He's given me these teachings so I can gently alert His people what really takes place and in a way that they will understand.

Yes, because that is being dropped out of the teaching now, about Hell and the Savior's suffering.

That's awful. But why?

Because they're scared of it. They don't want to think of it. Just like you were scared of it.

That's why they're pushing it off. Well, it does shake you up when He talks to you about the soul, doesn't it? So we push it out. We don't want to know truth.

Yes, and it's reality. It's out of love and mercy that He wants us to know the reality, because it's better for us to know it and not go to Hell, then not know it and go to Hell. You said that the sin is far greater because it's abusing grace. Then, you said something about the Holy Spirit, that He's the third person.

Yes, but He's God. He's in God. There's the Father, the Son, the divine Holy Spirit. They're three persons but they're all God, one God.

So He's the third person, and yet He's God.

The Father is God. The Son is God. The Holy Spirit is God. But They're three persons in the mystery.

And they're all equal.

The Holy Spirit was real loving to me. I can't describe how I relate to Him, but I love Him. And my love is growing deeper. He's getting closer and closer to me. I know I can't function without Him, and if I can't function without Him, He's part of my life, as a marriage. Remember that day He came into me? So He's very important in my life, and today He's making me feel this great love and this great need for Him. And the Father was delighted and Butchie was beaming all over because of this relationship with the Holy Spirit.

He's their Spirit.

Well, sure, He proceeds from the love of the Father and the love of the Son. He's a great Spirit. And this love is being infused into me.

And what did you say, it's almost like Mary —

Because what Mary became, she became through the infusion of the Holy Spirit. And I'm becoming what I'm becoming from the wisdom of the Spirit. Because I'm so dumb and stupid of myself, but what I give out is what the Spirit puts in me. He put into Mary Butchie, but He puts into me wisdom and the knowledge to speak my Father's word. Do you understand?

So as there was a marriage between the Spirit and Mary, there is a marriage between the Spirit and you?

But it's different, yet it's alike, because He's consuming me, and I'm putting out the Father's word, Butchie's word, which will bring life to people. Do you understand what I'm trying to say?

I do. And He said it's going to deepen more this Lent?

It's going to deepen more. I could feel it deepening today, because while I was talking to the Father, I could feel the Spirit coming to me. I could feel His life within me. The warmth, the peace. It engulfed the Father and the Son in me.

What experience did you have at the very end, when you were silent. Usually the Father embraces you at the end.

The Father embraced me, but it was all of us. It was like a cowboy's lasso thrown over us, reeling us in.

What was the lasso, grace or the Holy Spirit?

It was the Holy Spirit. It was a light, a powerful light, lassoing and reeling me into the Father and to the Son. There was just such peace there.

So did you end up…

In the embrace of the three Persons.

Of the three Persons. All three of them. That must have been quite an experience. Have you ever been embraced before by the three Persons at the same time?

Not all at once.

But this time it was all at once.

All at once. I can't explain it. It's the power, it's the light, engulfing the Father and the Son, and then, drawing me into them.

If you don't mind, I'd like to ask you about some of the lights you've been having about Mary and Gabriel.

There's nothing much, except my Father said Gabriel was Mary's constant companion.

Even before the Annunciation, or after the Annunciation?

After the Annunciation. He was her constant companion, and she loved him very much. She stayed very close to Gabriel. And then He told me about Adam being made out of the slime of the earth. So the new theologians, when they throw this out, don't know what they're talking about, because the Father's sticking to that. He said He made Adam out of the slime of the earth, but He said when it came to make a woman, He made her out of Adam's rib. He said He already began the dignity of woman.

So He was showing that what the Bible says is really literally true. He really did make Eve out of Adam's rib.

And He's also showing the dignity of the woman.

That she wasn't made out of the slime of the earth, but out of something greater.

Right. And He was paving the path for Mary. And then He brought me to Deuteronomy. I'll have to look it up. I've never read it. And He said nuns should wear nun's apparel because they have a dignity all of their own, and He wants to keep them in that role and dignity. Then He told me about Raphael. I always knew Raphael was a healing angel. But my Father said Raphael watched over and protected the Christ Child. When Butchie was in the Temple, and He was saying [*to Mary and Joseph*], "Didn't you know I'd be about my Father's business?" My Father said Raphael was there. He never left Him.

So He was there until the public life?

Right. Then He said, in the Garden of Olives, the angel that appeared to our Lord, to comfort Him, was Raphael. And He said it's not written in Scripture.

What about during the public life of our Lord when He was going around with His apostles for those three years?

What about it?

Was Raphael with Him then?

Raphael was His constant companion, because he was His protector. Michael is the protector of the tabernacle, but I never knew Raphael was the protector of the Christ Child.

Was he the protector of the adult Christ, too?

Yes, all the time.

What did he protect Him from, Satan?

Well, when He went up to fast and the devil tempted Him,

Raphael was the angel that came to comfort Him.

With some others?

My Father just mentioned Raphael.

That's beautiful.

Yes, but I never knew that. Thomasino knew it was Raphael. Thomasino tells me a lot of stuff. Thomasino knows a lot about angels, did you know that?

Yes, I knew that. He wrote a whole book *[a treatise]* on angels. How they think, and how they will, and how they move and what they do.

He did?

Yes.

How come I didn't hear about that book?

That's one of the reasons he's called the Angelic Doctor. What did the Father or Butchie say about Thomasino today? In your thanksgiving, you mentioned Thomasino.

Oh, Butchie dying on the cross. He said, Thomasino knew all of that.

He taught that?

Yes, He said he knew that.

Yes. I learned that from Thomasino.

You knew it? Then why are you listening to me?

It brings it back in a beautiful way.

You knew that?

Yes, Thomasino teaches that. But it's questioned now. Many theologians don't believe that Butchie saw each individual soul and died for each one *[individually]*.

The Father just said He did, and Butchie said He did.

The Father is showing that what Thomasino was teaching, that is being contradicted today, is true. That's important. It's just like with Adam and Eve, the Father's saying, Yes that's really true.

Did you know that the catechists can't mention angels to their catechism children? See, they're trying to throw Scripture out.

They're changing, reinterpreting Scripture.

Yes. That's not right.

So what else about Mary?

When Butchie was in His public life, you never hear anything about Mary. Mary would feel all the hurt, because she was all pure and all good, and all holy. She didn't have all these blockages that we have. My Father mentioned Siamese twins, when one gets hurt, the other is suffering. And my Father said that is how it was with Mary and Butchie. When He was suffering on the cross, physically, she was torn to pieces inside. Because of the love and the purity between them. He mentioned the Siamese twins because they were flesh of the flesh. Mary and Butchie were so pure, and so holy, Mary could feel everything.

His flesh was her flesh.

Yes. That's why she could feel everything that He was feeling. When they put the nails through His hands, Mary could actually feel the pains in her hands. My Father said there is more reality in the litany to the Mother of Sorrows than man has put into it. He said she has gone through the passion because she was all pure and all holy, and this was her flesh. What He felt, she felt. Flesh of my flesh. It gives you a whole different outlook on Mary. You love her. Of course you always loved Mary, all pure and all holy and all good. But to realize that she's gone through all the suffering... When He was spat upon, she felt it. When He was humiliated, Mary felt the humiliation. Not just because she was a mother, but because she was all pure and all holy before the Father. She was spotless, that's why she felt it more. There was no blemish in their love: no pride, no envy, no jealousy. There is no blemish in the love of the Father and the Son.

6. THE SOUL OF JESUS GOES TO THE FATHER
March 6, 1983

No, I love it here..... I don't mean to have a thoughtful look in my eyes, but I am thinking about something..... I'm wondering about You, Butchie..... Well, sit here on the rock, and I want You to answer me and tell me right now. Did You go to Hell?..... The Father said You didn't..... Well, because I wanted to hear it from You. When they put You in that cave, what did You do?..... **Your body lay there.** All right, when did You go to the Father?..... **Your soul went to the Father from the cross.** That's what the Father said.

Then what about these people who were waiting? What did You do about them?..... Well when Your soul went into Your body and You rose from the dead, they just rose with You?..... That's what the Father said.

And You asked the Father to take Your spirit on the cross? He took Your spirit, Your soul, right away..... But when You rose from the dead on the third day, they rose and started to come to?..... I understand. That's what the Father said, but we get all mixed up with this hell bit, Butchie. Hell is where the devils are. Right?..... **Right.....**

Yup, I don't care. I believe You. Anything the Father says. I just wanted to get it straight in my mind again..... Nope. It doesn't bother me as long as I go to Heaven. I don't care if they went or when, or what hour..... Nope, I'm not getting into that bit. I just wanted to ask You, so my mind could be at ease, not that it bothered me..... Nope, it never bothered me. I never dug into it.....

(laughs) No, I don't think I'm a big shot in preaching. I know what I'm capable of doing, and You know what I'm capable of doing. So we find peace there, right? ..... There's nothing else worrying me.

Oh, yes there is. I'm worrying about all these people leaving the Catholic Church..... Why are they leaving, Butchie? Why are they losing their faith?..... **They never had the faith to begin with.....** Then its very essential we ask to increase our faith every day..... The devil? He's the liar..... He tells lies..... The Father? ..... No, He told me that a lie travels halfway around the world before Mother Truth gets her boots on. That's how fast a lie can travel. So that's the devil, right?..... So, the devil's the liar and he moves fast..... Especially, when he knows there's a weakness in faith.....

Then it's very essential we tell Your people to pray for an increase of faith daily, right?..... **All these people came into the Spirit too fast.** But is it their fault, Butchie? ..... Why a baby falls out of bed? Well, nine times out of ten, it's because he's moved too close to the edge, and then he fell..... **And it's the same way with the people. They get into the Spirit too fast, and then they fall away. They don't have any foundation in the Spirit.....** I understand that. That's not too hard to understand.....

Teresa? Yeh, she was always falling down every time a priest walked by her.... **That isn't faith. Imagination.....** I think if somebody truly knows You and really loves You and experiences You, it would be different. So these people who are leaving, they don't really know You at all. 'Cause they could never do this if they did.

But then it puts a question to me..... They feel rich and full in Your love there. What am I going to tell them about that?..... **Their imagination. They are just seeking a different kind of outlet. They are not seeking Christ. They are seeking new adventures, but not in faith.....** I don't know if they'd accept that from me..... Carol? She said she found it alive there, more friendly, more loving..... **She didn't want to obey the rules of the Church.....** So this was her cop-out.....

But how could we put that across? I can't hurt them. I have to be very careful, Butchie..... **Tell them truth. Remember always, a lie is halfway around the world before truth even gets her boots** on. So lies travel faster than truth, especially in a religious group. Capi is lying to them in telling them there's more and richer fulfillment outside the Church. And they don't have the faith to begin with..... Well, I was real worried about that for sure.....

This union with You in Communion increases faith. It's one of the greatest professions of faith to receive You. That's really beautiful, Butchie. Then every time I go to Eucharist I'm professing my faith and it's growing? That's really great!..... Well, I never looked at it quite that way. I wanted to be so close to You and have You inside of me. And I wanted to receive You. You're right. It is the greatest profession of faith..... That's really neat..... Well, if You want me to say it, have the Spirit say it through me at the right time and in the right place.....

(laughs) No, Father. Butchie was telling me that the greatest profession of faith is to go to Communion in the morning..... Well, maybe I did know it. But I don't know if I knew it in that way, Father. I go because I love Him, and I want Him as close as I can have Him. But it is a great profession of faith. I'm professing my faith, leaving the house to go to church to receive Butchie.....

Well, no..... I have a tickle in my throat all the time..... Here. (coughs) Nope, it went down. (coughs) I'm glad You can't catch germs, Father. (coughs) You would be coughing all the time because of me..... Maybe I talk too much, my Father.

I have been asking Butchie a lot of questions..... I love You for sure. I am worried about the people You're losing, Father..... Really, Father. **We never had them in the first place.....** Yet they came to get the fullness of the Spirit..... **Infatuation.** I'm sorry, Father. I'm truly sorry about that. It must hurt You an awful lot. I know what You say in Scripture about being tepid..... I'm awful sorry, Father..... We didn't really have them, but I thought we did, and I felt so sad because we lost them. But you can't lose something you haven't got, right, Father?.....

Don't feel sad about it. We'll build up the faith of the people that come. We'll keep telling them to pray for an increase of faith and to profess their faith by going to Eucharist daily and receiving Butchie. That'll make them strong, Father, right? Don't feel sad any more. We'll keep them. We'll work hard and we'll pray and we'll fast, my Father, and we will teach them. Father, don't they know they're supposed to pray for an increase of faith?..... We will tell them, Father. And we will keep the ones we have, my Father.....

Nope, it never dawned on me that we didn't have them at all. I just thought we lost them, Father..... **They weren't solid in the faith. They were looking for new adventures.** But they could be strengthened by grace, Father..... **You have to be open first to be touched.....** Well then, Father, do You think most of the "Life in the Spirit" and awareness of the Spirit is just a new adventure for us Christians, or is the Spirit truly touching us deeply and overshadowing us?..... **Only if they truly change. The trouble with people is they don't know the great gift of faith.** But don't they have faith in their Church, Father?.....

Yes, the pendulum goes back and forth ..... Well, for sure. I prize being a Catholic, my Father..... I just think that I'm so unworthy that You called me. And yet, I feel very special in Your sight, Father..... Are You truly proud when I say that? You know I mean it from the depths of my soul, my Father. And that's grace working in me, right?..... And You teach me many things, and the Spirit gives me the light to understand them.....

If that's what You want, You will give me the wisdom to do it..... They have to know faith is a very special, wonderful thing. It has to be increased daily. Especially by Eucharist, receiving Butchie. And by acts of faith. They can be simple, like "I believe in You, Father. I truly believe in You, Father." That's enough?..... **Say it often, frequently, as much as possible.** That doesn't seem very hard, Father. I will tell them that. You must remind me what to say. I forget. Faith is very important, isn't it, Father?..... No, I feel pretty good about it now. I feel bad that they changed, and yet, I don't feel as bad realizing they never had it to begin with..... Yes, it's a precious gem, and we have to keep polishing it and polishing it and polishing it, and strengthening it, and admiring it and treasuring it and loving it. We have to talk to the Father about it and nourish it.....

(laughs) I'm glad I delight You. I wish I delighted myself. I get pretty sick of me sometimes..... Nope, I'm not dissatisfied with Your creation, Father..... I think I get bored with myself..... I don't think it's so funny, that it should get such a big laugh out of You. Not that big.....

This coming week? I will think about the faith. I will write down what You say, Father. 'Cause I know it's going to be very important. I promise You, my Father, I will write it down..... I'm glad You love me..... I love to hear You say it, Father. It makes me feel so warm and so secure..... No, I'll pray every day even more for a deeper, richer faith, Father..... Yes, for sure I will, my Father..... Faith is very special, a very priceless treasure.....

Puff, they can throw that in the jewelry box any time they want, but this will stay with me all the time, right?..... (laughs) I don't mean to be silly..... 'Course I love You, Father..... I love You more than anything in the whole world. And I love being with You all the time..... Yup, I will treasure it forever.....

INTERVIEW

He said that when He rose, He brought the holy people with Him to Heaven.

Right. Oh, you know what He said. When He put his head down, and He died on the cross His spirit, His soul, went right to the Father. No stops, right to the Father. And then He said, when I went to my Father *[that is, at the Ascension]*, the souls came with Me, because I opened the door to the Kingdom.

He said that the people who are leaving didn't have faith to begin with?

Right. I was so sad about them. And I said, Father, how come they're leaving the faith? He said, "Eileen, they didn't have the faith to begin with."

You said, but they seemed so spirit filled.

He said, "Well, that was just an emotional trip."

Why did He feel sad then. You didn't feel sad any longer, but He was still sad about it.

Because if they were in the Catholic Church, they would have a chance to be drawn to Him, and because they were not open to grace. Remember I said, "Well, couldn't You give them the grace?" And He said, "Eileen, they were not open to it." You know, we have to be open to it.

But you're going to open them to it.

I hope so, Father. You know what He said? "The biggest profession of faith is Eucharist."

That's beautiful.

Isn't that beautiful? I never thought of it like that. But then He also encouraged making acts of faith. "I believe in You, Father." You don't have to go through the whole Act of Faith. Just something simple, "I believe in You, God. I believe in You, my Father. I know You're there."

When you make an act of trust and surrender, that's an act of faith too.

Right. He doesn't go for big time words. No. Something very simple.

And He was telling you about people coming into the Spirit too fast, without a foundation. I think it is the way with people coming into contemplation too fast. They don't have the foundation. They haven't meditated on Jesus and His passion and sin. Remember, Jesus and the Father explained to you that they should be going through those stages and then He will lead them into contemplation. Remember?

Yes. You see, people that are in the charismatic movement know of the "Life in the Spirit." They all want to take it. And as soon as they finish it they think they know it all, they've got it all. But they haven't got the foundation. They have to have a deep prayer life. It's got to continue on the way home. It's got to be in their daily work. And they have to come to the sacraments. They have to know where they are and where they are coming from. They have to take time out to read the Scriptures.

Many of the charismatic people read the Scriptures from cover to cover and they think they have it, but they don't know Jesus at all. They don't spend time with Him. The Father said those people are like a child who gets into bed just at its edge, and easily falls out. Oh, you know what He said about a lie? A lie travels halfway around the world before Mother Truth gets her boots on. And He said, especially in religious groups. Because a lie is given by the devil, and he runs ahead with it.

And then He said something about an infatuation.

Well they're infatuated with the gifts. The Father said He was so pleased when I tell them that of myself I am nothing. "Don't look at me as a healer. I'm coming here to teach you and to learn with you, so we can be better people."

That's beautiful. So those people who get in too close to the edge of the bed, they're tempted.

Right. When they're getting into the Spirit, they're at the edge. They don't get into the middle of the Church where they should be with the sacraments, the rosary, the stations. They stay right at the edge. They don't go in deeper with Scripture and the life of a good Christian. They stay at the brink, they don't go into a deeper union with Christ.

So you asked Him what about this new awareness of the Spirit, is this just a new adventure?

Yes. He said nine times out of ten they're on an adventure trip. They want to see what they can get. Can they get tongues? Can they get prophecy? Can they get healing? Why? Because I want to be great. They're not looking for this deeper union with Jesus. The Father said, "Every time I bring forth something beautiful, the devil knows the weak spots." And the weak spots are: they want self esteem, they want to be showy. Then He said, the new awareness of the Spirit is from the Holy Spirit and is good only if they truly change.

That's right.

And so they need the gift of faith, a deepening of faith in order to really change and be converted. And that means that they're not acting for self esteem or to be a big shot by having the gifts. He said that's what the people see in me. He said, "You're not doing this for yourself, you truly want to bring people to Me, to know Me and to love Me." And I said, "Well, I hope so, my Father." He said, "Yes, Eileen, You won't change. You want to truly bring them to the Father." And He said, "They sense this. They sense the love you have for the Father, and they want that love." They're craving for it now. The Father told me that those who leave the Church are going for a good time. They go on picnics and all these things. And He said, "They're not going to find Me. They're going to where they can most live it up. They can find Me in the Church. They're not searching for Me, they're searching for their own gratification." They're going where everything is showy.

That's a beautiful explanation of what's happening.

Yes. And He said they are people of the pendulum. They're here and they're going to swing over to that faith and they'll swing back. They'll be going back and forth. Meantime the clock is going. The day will come, and they won't have their roots any place. That's frightening.

NOTE. *Catholic doctrine, based on certain Scripture texts, explains our Lord's descent into Hell to the souls of the just who were awaiting their redemption. St. Thomas distinguishes this part of Hell from the place where souls were undergoing purgation, and of course from the abode of the condemned souls. The Catechism of the Catholic Church* (French edition - my translation) says: *"Jesus did not descend into hell to deliver the damned nor to destroy the hell of damnation but to free the just who had preceded Him"* (First Part, Article 5).

The soul of Jesus, which had the divine vision during life (according to St. Thomas and Karl Rahner), *had this vision unimpeded after His death on the cross. Therefore His soul was immediately with the Father when He surrendered His soul to Him in death. When the risen Jesus ascended to His Father, the souls of the just accompanied Him. This revelation to Eileen corresponds to, and is to be understood in the context of, the Catholic tradition.*

7. "THEY WILL NOT KNOW THE PRICE"
March 13, 1993. Laetare Sunday

Eileen repeating the Father's words:

> I will work more gloriously for the Father
> And I will touch many hearts
> And I will bring many priests to Thee.
> And through the heartache and the pain
> The ministry will grow and bring glory
> To my Father.
> Yet they will not know the price
> One has to pay for their salvation.

8. A STAGE OF GROWTH
April 7, 1983

I wish I could tell them all about it. They would love so much to hear about it, Butchie. It would take them away from all worldly cares and troubles..... I have an escape, they don't..... **But they have to earn it.** I haven't earned it, Butchie. You just gave it to me for nothing...... Well, they're just sufferings that come my way, but I didn't think they were a price.....

It does? I don't think it could get any more beautiful than this, Butchie. Look at the way that stream flows. The gentle breeze that goes through the trees. Everything's in perfect harmony. You just feel the love. I could never earn such a place..... I don't think they would believe it anyhow..... Oh yes, I'm sure most people know a beautiful spot, but nothing like this, Butchie. Everything is just so perfect.

Even if I tried to explain it to them, it just sounds too beautiful. The fruit, everything is just too beautiful. Could they grasp it, Butch?..... I didn't think so. **First they must learn about You, and then the Father, and then the Spirit will overshadow them, and they'll have new enlightenments.....**

I was talking about that today, or was it yesterday, Butch? How we look for the Spirit, but mostly for what He can give us. Not for the depth of love for the Father. There is so much I want You to clear up in my mind, Butchie. But when I'm with You, I forget it..... Will He really do that for me?.....

I will tell Your people as much as the Spirit lets me tell them, and He'll give them the grace to grasp it..... Oh, you will reveal secrets here and there, and they will wonder where you got them. But won't that reveal my relationship with You, Butchie?..... Not if You say that's not wrong to reveal...... I don't know how special I am. I don't feel special. I don't think too much about it, except I'm scared *[before beginning to speak]*, and then it just comes out..... Of course it's the Spirit.....

But I would like them to see this place, to know what's in store for them, Butchie, to hear that brook singing. Listen to it. Its melodious tune..... They would think I'm a loony bird. To let them know that there's a peace here, a peace that touches the very soul. In my humanness, I feel like I don't belong here. And yet, You bring me, and of course I find peace in that. But I would like to share it with them, Butchie....

There's no time. No time to grow old. No time to fret. There's just the moment. It's hard to grasp. No time. Because if I had time, I'd be limited, right? And things would be over. So there's no time here. That is hard to grasp. I wouldn't know how to explain these things. Complete joy. Complete happiness. No searching. Always there. Always fresh. Always new. Never a letdown. Always the same. Yet exciting. Never dull.

I wouldn't know how to explain it, and yet, I want to share it. I feel the Spirit working within me even now. For He's telling me different things, and making me aware of a newness. Just this thing about time, Butch. I didn't know that before. There is no time. It's not that it stopped, it just isn't. Like the excitement, there's no end to it. And yet, not boring.

It's just unbelievable, so much beauty. Always drinking from it, more and more. Never quenching the thirst, but yet, no thirst. It just blows my mind. Your eyes are dancing with delight in my excitement and my new awareness of it all. To see it a thousand times, and yet, it's new. I can tell by Your face You're just delighted at this puzzlement of mine. Sure, it puzzles me. It's different.....

The Father? Yes, He said we can't even imagine what He has prepared for us. And today it's more beautiful than ever. The peace is here. Why do I see it differently, and yet, know there's more.....
The suffering of Lent. The Father said I would bear fruit from it.

And You're more beautiful than ever. I feel as though more veils have dropped..... More than one, for sure.

And when you send me back, I yearn *[to stay],* and yet I dare not yearn. I am not ready. There are many corners I have to polish, Butchie, so many things I have to do for the Father. I fear not death itself, Butch. I fear the time of meriting being over. That's what I fear, I guess. So, sure, I do yearn, and yet, I know there's time in my world to be a better person. I feel absorbed in the beauty, more deeply aware of the beauty. My soul feels light and I feel my spirit within me telling me that there's so much more. Even Your hand is warmer. Its lighter. Your steps are quicker. The love is deeper. Something great is taking place..... **The fruit of Lent.** I can't quite grasp it all. He's here now.

My Father, there's something taking place within my soul. No, not frightening, Father. It's beautiful and it's peaceful. My valley has more beauty, and I found there is no time. For time would mean a limit, an end, a beginning. It's always. I could not grasp this before. Not that it entered my mind, my Father. There is no time. There's always happiness without an end. And yet, not boring, Father.

I grasp it all at once, and yet I can't grasp it. It seems like it's trying to penetrate my soul, Father. Am I not ready for it, Father? Is Your Spirit not doing His work? Why can't I grasp it, my Father?..... That's what Butchie says, Father. For sure it was great, and it was painful. But Father, I looked for no reward. Thy face was all I wanted to see. I never expected all of this too, my Father. If only Your people could see this beauty, and feel the feelings I feel, my Father.....

But if You gave them the grace to understand it, Father..... But I do not look at it as a price, my Father..... Yes, Jesus paid a price..... **There's no seeing the Father without suffering.** Then the more one suffers for the love of her Father, her God, the more the Spirit takes

possession of her being. Who likes to suffer, my Father?..... No I
didn't ask for it, for sure. Maybe I'm a coward..... No, I don't refuse
it, right, Father. But I cannot ask for it, either, so therefore I think
I'm a coward..... Thank you, Father.

All this beauty for me, and I cannot share it..... But why
wouldn't they understand, my Father?..... **The sun comes through
the window, and it's rays hit the prisms of the lamp and they glow.
But its rays do not come through the window if the shade is drawn.
And that's the way it is with Your people. Those who stand in the
dark shadows of self cannot be touched by the light. We must expose our sins to the light of Your Son, and be deeply touched by
the Spirit.**

How I would love to share it, Father. I feel a new awakening.
I'm just so overwhelmed by it all, my Father. How many times I've
been in the valley, and I've never known this..... Yes, You did say
that. And Thomasino said that I would receive great teachings from
my Father. The element of time is important to us, Father, as humans... The Spirit will do that.....

Yes, I'm worried. I always worry before a talk, my Father..... I
trust You. I certainly trust the Spirit. Sure I trust Him. Would You
like me not to worry, my Father?..... Thank You. **I will say what He
wishes and the way He wants. And the people will be elevated towards their God. The teachings will be more powerful than ever.**

**Although I will not reveal my secrets, they will know I've been
in touch with my God. I need not speak of revelations, the Spirit
will lead me in such a way that they will know I've been in touch
with my God.....** No, it doesn't frighten me. It pleases me, because
I love the Father, and I do want people to know I'm in touch with
my Father. Not to know our intimate conversations, Dad, but to
know that I love You, to see the love that I hold for You in my face,
to know that the teachings come from the Spirit.....

Yes, Father, I will listen.

In your heart I will plant a new and deep way of communicating with My people, our people, our brothers and sisters. They will be touched deeply by the love you hold for the Father, the Son, and the Spirit, and they will be moved to lead better lives and bring glory to God. It will be a revolution, all for the glory of God.

Like an explosion, Father?..... Nope, I'm not frightened. I'm excited, Father, but my excitement is held back by the peace I feel within me. The peace that comes from my valley. The excitement is there from the things You have revealed to me today. Do you understand what I am saying, my Father? You know the secrets of my heart.....

I love You too, my Father. I love You so much that I would run to You in a moment and be with You forever. But I know You have work for me to do, Father. I know You would give in to me, because You spoil me. So I would not ask such a grace, or want such a grace. I will wait until you call me, Father, when the work You have for me is done..... Nope, I told Butchie, the only thing that frightens me in death is my time of meriting grace is over, and I want to please You. I need this time to please You more and more. But when You're ready, I'll certainly be so happy to come, Father.....

Thank You, Father. I love You so much, my Father. One look from You would be eternity for me, Father. All these other things are great, but just Your look is enough.

INTERVIEW

You would like to tell the people, show them what you're seeing? It is so much more beautiful because of the price you paid during Lent in suffering, just like Butchie paid a price?

Father, it's more beautiful than ever. The brook always sang, but it's like the singing has turned to a chime and the breeze kisses the shore as it goes by. And Butchie's more beautiful. And the atmosphere is more beautiful. My Father gave me an awareness for the first time: there's no time there. Because time would come to an end. He made me understand there's no time. It always is. Like the Father is. You're not bored. There's excitement without end. It's a living excitement, a living love. Something going on, and yet, not tiring.

So there's such beauty there that you want to share it?

I'd love to share it with my people, but my Father said they wouldn't be able to grasp it. They'd say, "She had a vision." Or a priest would say, "Oh, she's had a revelation." But He said it would be a fleeting moment of beauty to them. They wouldn't let it sink in. They wouldn't grasp it. It might come back to their mind as something beautiful, but they wouldn't understand it, and they would forget it. The Spirit will only reveal this when they are ready.

You wondered how it came to you. You didn't earn it.

No, I didn't. The Father can do as He pleases. I certainly didn't earn anything.

He said that they would understand that you were in touch with the Father.

He said they know. "Even now they know that you're in touch with Me, Eileen. They know there's something about you when you talk about the Father, that you love Him."

Because of an experience of Him.

Yes, because of an experience of the Father. But the depth of our love, they don't know. The Bishop said, "She truly loves the Father." But the Father said even he doesn't know how close we are.

I didn't know.

My Father said He's given you the grace to understand the relationship between my Father and me. But I thought you would never be able to understand it.

There were things that you wanted cleared up. And He probably said that the Spirit would clear them up when He was ready to?

It seems so unfair to keep all these beautiful things from God's people. If they knew there were so many beautiful things ahead, if I could reveal them to them, they would try to be so much better. And He said, "Eileen, this is a stage of growth in loving Me. You just can't jump into it. The Spirit will let you reveal to them what the Spirit knows they're ready for." But He said it's a stage of growth. One has to grow into it.

So, if you want to reveal it so much to them, and you can't, doesn't it give you give you any satisfaction that you can reveal it to your spiritual director?

Sure it does, and you understand.

And so, when I listen in, and hear it directly from you talking to Butchie, don't you see how meaningful that is because otherwise I could wonder: "She's telling me this. Is she trying to impress me?" But you don't even know I'm present when you're talking to Butchie. It's just you and Butchie. So, it gives me an insight then, and an assurance that's very important for a spiritual director. Do you understand that?

I think so. You should see how beautiful the valley is. Even more beautiful than before. There's no time, because time would mean fatigue, it would mean an end. There's no fatigue, there's no end. Early this morning when I was lying in bed and I was talking to my Father, I said, "Father, You've given me so much. I know I don't deserve it. I feel selfish." He's given me so much. So much love. And yet, when He withdrew from me during Lent, it was a withdrawal without knowing it was a withdrawal. It was a terrible thing. Harry was talking about that book, *Cloud of Unknowing*. And I said, "Harry. I hear many people talking about having been through a dark night. I'll be honest with you, they don't even know what they're talking about." Because if they went through it, they would never talk about it. It's just awful. They call me up and say, "I've been through a dark night but I knew He would come back, or He'd be there." And I said, "You don't know. There's no hope of getting out. It's an awful feeling. Hope would be the grace *[consolation]*. But there's not the grace *[consolation]* of hope there."

Harry might misunderstand that because actually you do have that hope. You can't feel it, you can't experience it. It seems like it's just empty. But it's a real act of hope that you're making, and the Father appreciates that, and there is real belief. But you don't feel it or experience it in any way, so it doesn't seem real to you. Harry might think you were despairing.

No, he didn't misunderstand that way. I couldn't actually say He was hiding, because I didn't have the grace to know He was hiding. It's like seeking and searching but not finding, ever. People will say, "I don't ever see the Father, He never talks to me." If you don't see Him, and He doesn't talk to you, the withdrawal isn't as deep as if you saw Him or He spoke to you. There are different depths to that withdrawal, and it's terrible.

So, then your Father came.

My Father said at one point, "Since Lent they're going to see something different in you when you talk to them. They're going to see a new depth to you. Each time they come, they keep saying, 'She's getting better and better and better.' This time they're going to see a deeper closeness and something new springing forth." He said, "The Spirit will show you what He expects of you, and you do it. Hold nothing back that the Spirit gives you. No matter what you think of it. Just say it."

Then you said at one point to the Father, "The Spirit will do that?" and "I'm always worried before a talk."

Yes, I did say that. He said He's glad that I do feel a little upset before a service. He said, "I'd worry more if you were too sure." He said when you depend totally and completely upon the Spirit, like I do — I know I have nothing — then the Father says, I listen. He never lets me do a service without Him. My Father is always there. And I want Him to be so proud of me. Knowing that I followed in the footsteps He wanted me to, in the Spirit.

9. STAYING BEHIND THE SHIELD OF FAITH
May 1, 1983

No, Butchie, it's not that I'm inquisitive. I'm very happy with what
the Father has told me already. I don't look for anything else. But
when the Father tells me things, of course I want to know what
He's talking about..... Why should You be amazed at the way He
deals with me? He loves me, doesn't He?..... Right..... You're not
supposed to be amazed at anything, Butchie, are You?..... Oh, it's
just that You're not used to seeing the Father deal with somebody
like this..... Sure, I feel privileged. I love Him. He's my Dad. And if
we can't talk, who am I going to talk to, Butchie?..... Yes, I understand that. It's because I'm used to talking to Him, and I don't
know what other people are doing. I only can relate to what I do, I
guess.....

Now, see that, even though You picked it, look, there's another one. That's hard for me to grasp..... (laughs) **I'm not supposed
to.** But I'm alert to what's going on, Butchie..... (laughs) I don't
mean to be funny, I guess I'm just inquisitive or nosey..... Of course
I do. That's a silly question. I love You with my whole heart and
soul. No, is it my soul or my spirit that I love You with?..... I'm
really amazed at the teachings the Father has given me, Butchie.....
I'm really loving You with my spirit. Loving You with my spirit
beautifies my soul. Right? (laughs) I think I've got it all together,
for today at least. I don't know about tomorrow. I'll probably get
lost unless You send the Spirit to come to my aid.....

I know. I feel as though it's a great mystery. I feel as though we
don't quite grasp everything the Father wants us to. And I'm thrilled
that He enlightens me through the Spirit to understand it...... That's
because He speaks to me in such an easy way, Butchie. You speak
to me so I understand, and the Spirit makes me understand.....
Nope. I think I have it straight..... Well, I really don't read what

they talk about, Butchie. I just know what You and the Father say, and I'm not going to discuss it with them. I don't want them to think I'm a heretic..... (laughs) I don't quite know what it means. Going against Church faith, I guess..... Yes, I got that clear.

You never went to Hell. I didn't think You'd go there in the first place..... Yes, I understand that. Well, that's what we were talking about, Butchie..... Yes. **Your spirit went into the Father's hands, and there was a reunion and a love time. And then You went to quiet the people down, to give them hope.** Right..... Well, that's what I understood from the last time.

There's so much that we don't understand, Butchie. Do You think it's our fault? Maybe Your Spirit isn't coming down upon us as powerfully as He should. And I don't mean to complain about You, Spirit, but all of a sudden You seem to be doing a good job. What were You doing before?..... Nope, I'm not criticizing You. I'm just wondering how come all the lights are coming now..... **Nobody speaks to You like that.** Well, I don't mean to be naughty, for sure, I'm just wondering how come You're working overtime..... (laughs) I love You for sure. You know I love You, and You know how much I depend upon You for my services and everything. And I'm not giving You holy moly. That's a good word for heck, right?.....

I'll be content with the light I'm getting now, but I can't help wondering what You were doing before..... Look, even Butchie is grinning, but He loves You. For sure He loves You. And I love You. I know I'm no good without You..... Yes, that's what my Father says. You've got to give me a lot of light now, listen, because I want to understand this spirit and soul bit. Right, Butch?..... Right. See? You're the third person, You've got to get going..... Well, I think it's pretty super. I always said my soul when I really meant — well I didn't mean it, because I didn't know it. See, there You go again, You didn't give that light to my spirit..... Right, I under-

stand that now, and that's because You're doing Your job.....
Nope..... I do love You for sure..... I didn't even know about that
shield of faith. What were You doing when I was supposed to know
this stuff..... **One thing at a time.**

I'm glad You're giving me the light now to understand my Fa-
ther's word. I have to pray for a stronger shield, a stronger faith.
Then I'll be protected from all the arrows of anxiety, frustration.
Even from this attack on me in the past day or two, right?..... **Right.**
So that shield of faith protects me from this. I have to believe I'm
doing the right thing, and I'm pleasing my Father, right?

And what else?..... **Pray for that person.** How does that
strengthen my faith and protect me from getting wounded?.....
Because I would have been wounded by an arrow of hate. Ah ha!
Now I know what You mean. By making acts of love, I strengthen
my faith, and the faith is the shield that protects me from this terrible arrow of hate..... See? You gave me the light then..... Right. I
understand more about the shield now..... Great..... How come
nobody ever told us about this..... Good thing I have the Father.

Butchie, did You know all this stuff?..... How come You didn't
tell me?..... **Only the Father says when I'm ready to know things.
He's the only one that will give me the revelations.** And that's a
revelation? Great. Then the Father is really the big shot..... Listen,
Butchie, I don't want to get into that Trinity bit, I get too confused.
I love You, and I love the Holy Spirit, and I love my Father, and
we'll let it go at that. It's hard enough to understand the body, the
spirit, and the soul. Don't start me on the Trinity right now. I take
it the Father is the boss. He's the first person. He's Daddy God. I
understand that, and we're going to leave it there, OK?..... For sure.
At least we're in agreement.....

Right. We'll ask the Father..... I don't mean to be funny, Butchie, I just want to get everything in order, and You know it's kind of
a slow train for me. I've got to really weigh it out..... Yes, I under-

stand it now, I'm sure..... Yes, thanks to the Spirit..... Right. I don't
think we as humans understand all of this, Butchie. I don't even
think some of our priests understand it. They say we have a body
and a soul. And that's good. They don't tell us anything about a
spirit. Just as I was told that the Father doesn't have a body. And
the Father says slow down now, read your Scripture. First He wants
to keep me out of Scripture, now He's telling me to read the Scripture.....

(laughs) I knew You were listening, my Father..... Nope, I'm
not complaining. You're just telling me that there's proof of it in
Scripture. I understand that, my Father. What I don't understand,
Father, is how come we don't hear about the body, the spirit, and
the soul, just the body and the soul..... But You tell us not to dig
too much into Scripture, then what's this all about?..... **We're not
reading it right**..... Well, it says if anybody sees God they will die.
I'm still kicking, Father, I see You..... Yes, I know there are many
veils between us. I also know that You drop the veils and You're
more beautiful than ever at different times. You get more beautiful and more beautiful. But I understand, my Father, there's so
much more. It's a feeling within, and that feeling is You within my
spirit.....

Yes, I understand about Your making us to Your image. I don't
think many of us understand that, Father..... Yes, I think it's deep
for us as humans. It's deep..... Well, it may be clear there, but sometimes, even being clear, it's as clear as mud..... You gave me the
light, that's why I understand now, Father. If You didn't give me
the light of the Spirit, I wouldn't understand anything..... **You're
going to tell me more about the spirit, and the soul, and the
body.....**   Oh Father, when am I going to get the time to tape.
I don't mean to complain. I know You want it on tape, but the
time is just not available, my Father..... I will do it the first chance I
get, Father. And I do look for chances..... No, I don't want to lose

any of this teaching..... Well, it's getting warmer, and I will go out there.....

It's very important that I speak of faith, body, spirit, and soul. It's very important that man knows what he's made of..... I do, I think it's very important. I just think it's neat having the shield of faith, protected from the darts of hatred, anger. I believe, and I strengthen my faith by believing, and the shield gets thicker, and nothing can touch me..... **But I must stand behind the shield of faith, because if I expose myself, I will get wounded.....** What does that mean, that if I step outside of my faith? How can I step outside of my faith, my Father?..... **Easy.** Oh boy. What do You mean by easy, Father?..... **Loose doctrine..... And if I don't stand firm on doctrine, I'll step outside of the shield, and I'll get wounded, even to the point of death.** Then it's important, my Father, that I stand strong behind the shield of the faith You have called me to, Father. Then I'll always be protected.....

All right. **As a human, and as a Catholic, I stand behind the shield within my Church, and I must not be inquisitive, and I must not lean outside, because if I lean outside of the shield, I'm going to get it.** I understand, Father. I know just what You're talking about, and I feel the Spirit working within me, Father. I can't lean toward a different faith, not even to appease them, Father, because I'll be leaning outside the shield, and I'll be wounded. And that's what is happening to our priests. They're leaning too much, and they're getting wounded. They're not behind the shield of faith.

That makes a lot of sense. Father, You're a smart guy..... Of course I think so. Look at how great You teach me, Father. You're the smartest..... What do You mean You like to think so? You know so. You're God. You're just being a clown today, my Father. I think I had enough of it with the Spirit today. It's rubbing off on You, Father..... Of course I love You. I love You more..... I think my heart would burst if I loved You any more. And yet, I know I'm going to love You even more, although it seems impossible at this point..... (laughs) Do I sound like a contradiction, Father? How do You put up with me?.....

When You say You love me, I feel it sinking into me deeper and deeper. It's like dropping a pebble from the top of a mountain into a stream. I-love-you falling deeper, deeper, deeper, deeper..... It's just super..... I love to have You teach me, Father. I feel alive when You teach me, Father..... Well, I felt pretty dead last night. I just can't find a reason for it. And I don't want to think about it because I want to love that person, my Father. But You can't blame me, Father, for hating the action..... You hate it too? You mean there is something You can hate? You hate the actions? I thought hate wasn't in Your vocabulary, Father..... I understand the way You're using it..... Well, no, I didn't feel a bit of hatred for them. I felt sad because I couldn't understand it, Father.....

You did? You felt sad too?..... Nope, I don't like You to feel sad. It's bad enough I get clobbered..... Well, I hope You don't get clobbered any more then..... Nope, I can truly pray for that person. I just can't justify what they did. But there might be something wrong with them. Maybe they haven't got all their marbles..... Of course I can pray for them. II do, Father, and I'll continue to do so..... But anyway, I'm very happy for what You teach me. I'm not trying to change the subject. But I just don't want to talk about that any more because I don't want to make You sad..... Nope, I think mine has gone by. Thank You, Father.....

Are You really going to teach me more about the soul, the spirit and the body? Is there a lot more to know, my Father?..... What are You going to teach me about that?..... Not now? Now You're teasing me, Father..... And You're going to leave it like that? You're not going to tell me? You're just going to leave me hanging? You're teasing me now, see?..... Of course I mind, but I'll go along with it..... Nope, I love the way You said You took a form. Sometimes if

I would let it slip, they'd say I'm a dodo bird. But I know my Father, He can do anything He wants.....

Then it's true. You were sitting on the throne, and You did have a right hand. So see, I'm not such a loony bird, Father..... Nope, I knew I wasn't, but sometimes people think I am, and that's why I don't tell them too much, Father.....

Nope, I won't tell him. Did You see what He said this morning, Father? He said, "Ask the Father about Yugoslavia" *[Medjugorje]*. I said, "No, I'm not going to ask Him. If He wants to tell you, He'll tell you Himself." And I'm not asking You, Father, and I don't want You to tell me anything, my Father. Right?..... Right. You just do what You want to do, and I'll have faith, and I'll pray..... He wanted a whole message from You, Father, and I said, "No way. I don't think it's right to ask the Father." Are You happy with that answer, Father?..... Good.

I love You, Father, and I love him, but I think he uses me as a fortune teller, Father. He wants to know the present and the future, and I know You don't want that of me, my Father..... Well, I think I know the difference between a mystic and a fortune teller. I'm pretty sure I do, my Father. But he's a priest, and he should know the difference. This is about the third or fifth time he's asked me to do this, Father..... Father, I love You, and I don't want You to tell me anything about it. I want to go by faith and prayer.....

I know You would, my Father, but we'll leave it at that, all right? You loving me, and I trusting You..... I'll remember that, Father. **There is more to faith than meets the human eye. There is more to the spirit and there is more to the soul. I will give to thee great revelations, and they will be brought forth in the light when you are with Me for all eternity.....**

All right..... Nope, I'm not afraid. Father, if You're with me, who cares who's against me. I may hurt for a sliver, like last night, but then I have You to run to, my Father. That's all that I care about..... I love You so much too, Father..... Yes, I long to be with You, but I know You have work for me to do, and that's OK..... As long as You keep sending that Spirit to me, Father. Sometimes I think He's on strike..... He doesn't strike? Then how come He's overtime now?..... Do You think I'm being hard on Him, Father?..... (laughs) **He delights in it.** I love Him, for sure. I know I wouldn't be able to understand anything, Father, except for the Spirit. And I'm just teasing Him about being on strike. He knows that I love Him, right, Father?..... Right. I love You so much, I justwanteveryone to love You, Father. Everyone, everyone, everyone.

INTERVIEW

So the Father said He's going to tell you more about the body, soul and spirit?

Right. It's a real big thing to know He says.

He says man should know about himself?

Right. Man should know about himself.

And then He explained something about the shield of faith, and how it was protection because of the arrows of hatred and anger, and how by prayer and by loving these people you strengthen your faith?

Yes, He did. And I strengthen my faith by saying I believe, I trust in the Father. He's going to bring good out of this. I didn't step outside the shield and get into despair, then the arrow of hate would have hit me. I'd be stepping outside of faith, away from that shield. That's such a beautiful teaching.

How do you step aside?

You step aside by saying, "Now, why did she do this to me?" All the time you're dwelling on it you are getting away from your faith. Instead of questioning, say, "Father, I know You're going to draw some good from this. I know You are." And you're staying within your faith.

When you say that, you're really remaining in faith?

Right, and you're strengthening it. But if I step outside of faith and said, "Well, that's the end, I tried to do good" that poison arrow could get into me, and I'd start building up hatred, because I stepped outside of believing.

And then you also said that by standing strong in doctrine, you stand behind the shield?

Right. You stand behind the faith, but if you lean too much towards other faiths, you're going to lean outside that shield, and you're going to get struck down, because you're getting away from the shield of your own faith. That's what's happening to many priests. Wasn't that a good teaching?

That was a beautiful teaching.

I wish He'd give it to me for His people, and let some priests hear it.

He doesn't want you to lose these teachings. He wants you to put them on tape. And He says that you'll have time to do it now, with the better weather.

Right. He said with the better weather.

Did He say anything about telling your spiritual director about it, so you wouldn't lose it?

He told me you were listening. And I looked around. He said, You know how he's listening. And I thought, Boy, this guy hears everything. He's lucky we let him in on my valley. And the Father read my mind and He giggled.

But weren't you glad your spiritual director was listening?

I guess. You know he's listening but you look to see him, and you can't see him.

Oh, you couldn't see him?

No, I couldn't see him.

He didn't show you that he was listening. He just told you.

Nope, I couldn't see you. I realized what my Father was saying, and I turned to look but I couldn't see you. You weren't there. That was a good teaching about faith. Wasn't that nice?

That was a beautiful teaching. He said it was easy to step outside the shield.

He says when you're leaning too much toward the opposite faith, these other religions, you get away from the shield, and you're open to being wounded by temptation, aggravation, acts of not believing.

You lose . . .

True doctrine. Sure, because you're leaning too much outside, and you're not protected by the shield of faith. That was a nice way of putting it. He's pretty smart, my Father.

10. THE WAY TO RENEW THE CHURCH
May 25, 1983

I know it will be renewed, Butchie, but I don't like to hear about it. You sound like a politician, always talking about the Church. I like to talk about other things..... No, everything. The birds, the brook, the beauty..... How can this go with the Church?..... Oh. Then if they don't build up the Church, they can't have any of this, right? Then what are You going to do, put them all in Hell?..... He said there will be but a handful *[of good Roman Catholics left].*..... What about the ones that have died and weren't in the Church. Well, not in the real Church. You didn't put them in Hell..... Tough, Catholics, if they're not good Roman Catholics, they won't come here? What if they're pretty good?..... Well, what if they obeyed the Ten Commandments, and went to Church?..... That would make them real good? They wouldn't be pretty good, then?..... Yes, I know the Commandments..... Yes. It contains just about everything. Then they'd be good, right?.....

Well, I think it's awful hard to be a Catholic..... Oh, maybe not for You, because You're all good, but remember where we're coming from, Butchie. We're not all good..... Oh, we want to be, but we're not all there..... Well, look at how many times I say, "I'm sorry."..... Yes, I do say it..... For sure I know I couldn't say it without grace and acceptance of grace..... I told them about that Sunday, that we take the word "grace" for granted. Were You happy?..... Well, it seems like You're going to tell me whether I want to listen or not, so I guess I better listen, because You won't talk about anything else.....

(laughs) I don't think I'm a hard nut to crack. I just like to talk about other things..... I know it's very important, Butchie, but You know, when I come here, I don't like to talk about all that stuff. I get so much of it all day long, Butchie. You just want to drown me in it..... (laughs) Thank You. I didn't mean drown, but You know what I mean. Sometimes I get tired of talking about all this stuff, I just want peace..... **I'll never have it unless the Church is back in order.....** I don't know how one person can do all of that. Certainly not me, for sure. I get clobbered, Butchie, for no reason. You want me to get my head on a platter..... Nope. I guess it wouldn't matter, as long as You brought it here..... You're funny.....

OK, You talk and I'll listen..... **A revolution.** Like a war? **A turning point. And it's going to be either for the good or for the worse, there's going to be no in between.....** Then the good people will follow You, Butchie, and the Father?..... **Through the Church.** What Church?..... No, I'm not trying to be funny..... Then there will be no happy medium. It'll either be the good Church, or it's going to be the "fallen away Church," the liberals. There is going to be no in between during this revolution, right?..... **Those that think they're in between will be out of the Church.** Will they know they're out of the Church, or will just You know?..... Yes, I understand that. I want to understand it all..... Well, they're not going to listen to me..... Nope, You never did. You never will. So I'll listen.....

Of course I know You love me. That's why I want to stay here and not talk about that stuff..... It seems lately, Butchie, every time You call me here, You're talking about the condition of the Church. I know its condition, and You know its condition, so let's not talk about it..... I don't see what I can do..... The services, that's all..... Oh, if I go on Tuesday. I don't care about going. Of course I'll go if He inspires me. I won't fight it.....

You know, Butchie, Your Mother's appearing all over the place, can't You start appearing on the altar and let people see You're for real too? Why are You letting Your Mother do all the work? Why don't You do something about it in the Eucharist?..... You mean the healings? But You've got to give them credit, they're taking it by faith. But if You popped Your head out of the tabernacle. See how they're rushing all over. They'd rush to see You..... Well, I know that, but still, the Blessed Mother's appearing, doesn't she know that, about faith and believing and not seeing? Well, can't You do something for these people..... You said before You would give signs in the Eucharist..... I know, but to me. I can't tell anybody that stuff. You don't want me to tell anybody that stuff. Then why don't You just pop Your head out and say hello. Then all the priests would come to that church to say Mass, and they'd be better priests and better people.....

I'm not being silly. Your Mother's doing it, and she's converting people in different places..... Yes, I know all about the Sacred Heart. They didn't stay converted. Then You're not commenting on Mary, your Mother, appearing, right? Why won't You comment on it?..... No, I don't think I'm nosey, I just want to know about this stuff..... Butchie, I love You. I'm not telling You what to do. You know that. But we need some kind of sign. We're only human beings. Look how they're traipsing all over the place. Garabandal and now this other place *[Medjugorje]*. We're humans, and we look for human signs, Butchie. Couldn't You just give a couple..... I know, but I can't tell them that, Butchie..... But is it enough for me to see?..... They are? They know something? What did they say?.....**This woman sees God.** I think that's beautiful, but don't You think they get jealous if they really think that? Don't You think they want to see You too? I would be jealous.....

I don't mean to be a tough cookie, I just want to know why You're not doing it..... **Because when people are converted by visions, the visions pass away, and then it's not a true conversion. But if they're converted by a deep faith, trust and believing, then it will last forever.....** You mean just going to the Eucharist, and not seeing You but believing with all your heart and searching for a deeper faith, then this faith will last forever..... **Even more than all those visions and apparitions.....** This is solid stuff..... I understand what You're saying..... Yes, I understand that, but I think they would like to see You stick Your nose out once in awhile, at least just once..... **But they would forget.** That makes a lot of sense..... Yes, I say that over and over. **With all the apparitions and visions, the world hasn't been converted, and it still won't be, even if You walked up and down the altar twice a day. But it's the deep faith, and not seeing, that converts the world.....**

Well I believe You because You said it, but I'll have to think about it. Do You mind?..... (laughs) Thank You. I'll have to do some heavy thinking about that one. But I'll come back if I don't understand it, for sure.....

(laughs) I see it. There's a bird in the middle of that flower. Is that a lily pad? It looks like our lily pads..... **A tasha.** What's a tasha?..... **The flower is a tasha.** Why do You call it tasha?..... **Smile of the Father. It means He smiled and the flower was there. Tasha.** How do You spell it?..... **There's no spelling.** How can you remember? Why don't You spell?..... **You will it.** (laughs) Well, don't You have any dictionary? Who made up all the words?..... Tasha. Tasha. I don't understand You. **There are no words here that are spelled. There are no dictionaries here.** Yet, that's a tasha. You are funny. I don't know how You expect me to get along up here, I can't even get along down there..... Thank You..... (laughs)

Tasha. I'll remember, I hope..... He looks like he's just taking a ride for himself down the stream, independent as ever. Look, he looked at You and He bowed to You. Look at how he is Mr. Bigshot, Mr. Cool. Will he fall off?..... See, that's what I like. I don't like talking about politics..... **It's not politics.** Well, whatever You say, but I don't like talking about it. But I'm glad You told me about the faith. Faith is better, and it will last forever, and these visions and apparitions will all fade away. And they really won't turn the Church around. They never have, and they never will. I remember that much. But if we go to You, and we kneel before the tabernacle, even if You decide to stay in and don't look at us, then this faith can go on forever and ever, and it's more meaningful than the other..... I don't know. If You say so..... I wouldn't like You to disappear on me, behind that door..... Nope, I don't question. I just take it and accept it.....

(laughs) You never give me the complete, full answers that I want, nor do You give me the satisfaction of doing what I want. You always make me do what You want, but You never do what I want..... Well, I'd like You to stick Your nose out to some of Your priests..... Why wouldn't it do them any good?..... How could they not believe it?..... **You'd have to do it every day of the week.** Well, wouldn't once be enough, Butchie?..... Our Blessed Mother?..... I guess not. I don't know..... Nope, I'm not going to bug You to do it. If You want to be stubborn, that's up to You..... Well, if I did it, You'd say I was stubborn..... You can do what You want. You know better than I do. You're a lot smarter, for sure. And if You say this is the way to change the world and for it to be converted, then You must know what You're doing. You're the Father's Son..... (laughs) I'm glad You remember I'm Your bride..... Yes, I'm the Father's daughter.....

No, Father, there's no doubt in my mind that I'm Your daughter. We're just having a little battle here..... Well, I told Butchie He wants me to do everything He wants me to do. And I asked Him to do one little thing, stick His nose out of the tabernacle to His priests, and He says He's not going to do it..... Well, I thought it would change some of them..... Well, Butchie, tell the Father what You said..... All right, I'll tell Him. He says it wouldn't make any difference, Father, because when He appeared as the Sacred Heart, the world changed for a while, but it didn't completely change the world, nor did the appearances of His Mother. So He says change has to come from a deep faith. Just kneeling, trusting, and trying to believe and understand. We're not at that point. Then this will be the success of light: faith in the Father and the Son and the Spirit..... Well, I have to believe Him, He's Your kid..... I know He's my spouse, but I believe Him because He's Your Son, and He couldn't be Your Son if He told a fib.....

I don't understand it, my Father..... If I don't understand, why are You telling me all this stuff?..... Sometimes You talk in riddles..... Of course I love You. I always love You. Even when I don't understand, I love You, my Father. But if Butchie says that's the way to renew the Church, to believe with all Your heart and soul that Jesus Christ is alive in that tabernacle, even if you don't see Him, then I guess that's the way to renew the Church..... Of course I'm glad I see Him. My heart breaks when I don't, Father..... Is that because I have a mission?

I think I see my mission clearer than ever, Father. I saw it when I was all by myself at night in the room. You sent Joan to me, and she told me that I was going to suffer and that I'd be wounded. That's the first time You sent her to me, my Father. She said somebody has to come to renew the Church.

You must get awful tired of us. Is a century a blink of an eye to You, Father?..... Then it would be almost every day somebody has to come..... Nope. You tell me I will be like a mighty warrior. Nope, I didn't tell anybody the dream. You know I didn't. I wouldn't tell anybody that. I'd be afraid they'd think I was being pompous, a big shot. I wouldn't dare tell anybody what You said, Father..... She said I would ride a white stallion of faith. She told me again about that shield, and that's why I used it [in her teaching], Father. But I didn't apply it to myself, because I didn't want them to know anything..... She told me I would be wounded by many arrows, by persecution. That I would bleed heavily in sorrow and pain, sometimes in depression, but she said I wouldn't get down from that stallion.....

I couldn't quite understand what she was telling me. But I understand it now and I'm sure it's the Spirit..... Of course I love the Spirit. I wouldn't understand any of this stuff. I would think I was as cuckoo as a dodo bird..... I'm not going to question it, Father. I'm sure You'll bring it about as You wish..... She told me, or rather, she showed me, my Father, that behind me, there would be all these priests upon their stallions, and they would be following me, and they would be persecuted, too..... Yes, my Father, I understand what she's saying. They will be the priests that want doctrine, tradition, and discipline in the Church. Right, Father? And the ones that would be fighting [us] would be the liberals..... I never thought liberals could give us that much trouble, Father. Well I know they're pulling the Church in different directions, but I didn't think they would actually make war on us, Father.....

Capi? I know he's angry with me. That's a good sign, right?..... Well, he torments me now, I don't know what else he could do..... Really? Lots? Well You better tell Michael to mind his business and stay close to me, or I'm not going to talk to him any more. He's the only protection I've got against that dopey Gillis.....

Joan?..... I guess I love her, Father, but she's a real hard looking person. She doesn't have softness in her face..... But she was stern with me, Father..... No, I'm not going to tell anybody. I would never say anything like that. I would sound like those terrible letters [arrogant letters berating the priest to whom they were sent, bearing her forged signature and not in her handwriting]. No way, it's enough that I know it. I can't quite figure it out yet, Father, but if You say it's right and that You sent her, certainly I believe it.....

My tongue?..... It doesn't feel like a sword. **It'll be a mighty sword that cuts through** — how can you cut through a liberal with a tongue that doesn't even look like a sword, Father?..... **Words that the Holy Spirit puts there will cut through all their doctrine and false teachings, and clear them away. It will slaughter them, and the truth will shine.** I don't know if I like this kind of stuff.....

Your tongue will be like a sword. It will be sharp, and it will cut through false doctrine and false teaching in the Church. And it will be like striking a warrior. And the liberals will bleed and fade away. And the Father will come through in force and in truth. And the Church shall rise and be glorious before the Father.....

I'm listening, Father. Boy, You've got big plans..... I know You have the power to do it, Father. You can do anything You want..... How could I love You less for using me? I love You more, but I hope You know who You're dealing with. I love You so much, Father. My only fear is that I'm going to let You down, and I don't want to let You down, my Father. You seem to have such high hopes for me. You better send that Spirit to come upon me..... Of course I love the Spirit..... I know I'm not capable of doing anything without Him. You know my secrets, Father, and You know I tell truth, that without the Spirit I would be a jellyfish, nothing.....

I'll remember that, Father, I'll remember everything Joan said to me..... Yes, my Father..... Well, I don't mean to look that way. I'm just listening so intently, Father..... Well then I can't fail, if You're with me, how could I fail?.....

Joan told me of all the attacks..... Of course I hurt, my Father, You know I hurt. It took me so long to forgive them, and to pray for them [*the woman who composed the forged letter and her confederate*], and now I've got to begin all over after what they said again..... I remember, Father..... On the pillow of the Father's chest I will rest. No friend or foe can reach me. He has placed upon me a mighty armor, and only He has the key to unlock me..... I'm thrilled to death over it. Only You have the key to set me free.

INTERVIEW

You were struggling with Butchie. He wanted to talk about the Church, and you . . .

I didn't want to talk about the Church. He's turning into a politician. All He wants to talk about is business. I like to play. And if Mary appears all over, why can't He stick His nose out just once and see if He can change us around? He said, "Eileen, I appeared as the Sacred Heart. They were fascinated for awhile. Some still look at me as the Sacred Heart, but did it change the world? No. My Mother came down and appeared to people and has it changed the world?" I said, "Well, You've told me that before, but she's still doing it, why can't You do it just once? Just once stick Your nose out of the tabernacle?" He said, "I'm revealing myself to you, am I not, through the Eucharist?" I said, "But I can't tell people this. They're not going to listen. And if they listen, they aren't going to get it."

He shows Himself to you because you have a special mission.

He said, "Eileen, believe Me, they know you see Me. They want to get deeper into what you're saying because they know you know something about the Father and Me. They see it in your face." And He said, "It's better to believe by faith, and the faith lasts. The visions and the apparitions don't last. People forget them. That's their humanness. But if they get down and kneel and beg for an increase of faith, and truly work at it, this kind of faith lasts forever. It doesn't fade away." All these supernatural things fade away, because we're human.

That's a good answer, isn't it?

Yes. He always has good answers. One thing I can say about Him, He's always got the answer. He always wins.

He's supposed to have. He's a teacher. You don't want the teacher to be dumb and not have the answers.

He's far from dumb. He knows everything.

So, who was it that explained your mission to you? Who was that lady? You're talking to your spiritual director now, and the Father said you should tell him everything.

Joan.

Was it Joan of Arc?

Yes. How did you know?

I guessed.

Yes. She never appeared to me before.

Is she friendly with you now?

Yes, but she's got a severe face. She's by no means gentle.

But she was young when she died.

But she's got a hard face. She knows her stuff.

She really means business. She's a warrior.

Yes, she means business all right.

So what did she say?

That I would ride a mighty stallion of faith in this terrible trial of the Church, and that I would have the shield of faith to protect me. But she said I will be struck by many arrows and that I will bleed, and it will be the liberals making me bleed, and the priests that are not walking in the light of truth. But she said behind me I will gather many warriors of priests and they'll mount the stallions of faith, and they'll be my protectors. And she said by their good example, when they march after me, other priests are going to join this army, and they'll be the protectors of the Church.

She led an army, herself, Joan, to free France from the British.

She didn't say that.

That's what happened. She was just a girl of nineteen, I think, when she led an army [actually seventeen]. A nineteen year old girl raised an army and defeated the British to free France, to liberate it. She wore armor, and led the soldiers in battle.

My Father said neither friend nor foe will be able to reach me. He will unlock my armor and set me free when I'm ready to go to Him.

He said your tongue would be a sword.

Yes, He said my tongue would be a mighty sword.

Is that because the word would be on your tongue?

That's what He said. He said, "You will pierce them with the word of the Holy Spirit." And they're not going to like what I say. They'll make me bleed, and they'll make me hurt, and they might even fill me with sadness.

He said you might have depression, but He said, you won't be thrown from your horse?

Right. And He said my sword will cut right through the liberals who are doing an awful job on the Church.

And you didn't know that the liberals were at war with the Church, that they're the opposing army, and they're led by Capi?

Yes. And they're not the people outside. It's the liberal priests and sisters who are doing a job on the Church. Sunday I told the people that a priest came to me and said, "Eileen, how do you know that God isn't the Mother instead of the Father?" And I said, "When Jesus was in the Garden of Agony, He said, 'Father, take this cup from Me.' And He said, 'I've come to reveal my Father.' Now, *father* is masculine. He didn't say, 'I've come to reveal my Mother. Mother, take this cup from Me.' He didn't say, 'Mother, into thy hands I commend my spirit.' He said, 'Father.' So God is masculine, He takes the appearance of a masculine gender. But God balanced the scales, He gave us Mary, a mother for Jesus, and we're to relate to Mary.' But I said to this priest, 'You better get back into Scripture and read it.' " I told the people that he was a well meaning and a learned man, but he's getting loose in his theology. He's turning into a liberal. And I said, "He was the same one that said to me, God has no body. Why do you relate to Him as Daddy and Father? He is a Spirit." And I said to him, "Go to John, he says, 'I saw Him sitting on a throne.' Now, if He's sitting on a throne, He had a rump." And they all laughed.

Where was this?

At St. John's. I said, "If He's sitting in a chair, He has to have a rump. And He has a hand, because John said, in His right hand He had a scroll. If He had a right hand, He had a left hand, and do you think he'd sit there without any feet, and just two arms?" And the priests were going like this, "You're right, You're right." I said, "You know, this was a learned man, and he means well, but he's tearing things apart. He's listening to the liberal theology that's coming into the Church, and he is stepping outside the shield of faith." I showed them the podium. I said, "This is my shield of faith. My shield. It's protecting my body. The moment I lean outside of my faith, the devil has his arrow on me and he's going to wound me." And I said, "If that's what you want to do, take chances with your faith by going to a Protestant church and participating in their services — you're not equipped for it. Get out of there."

Did your Spouse say that only a handful of Roman Catholics would be Catholic?

That's right. He said, "In every century the Church has to clean out because false teachings have come in. In every century there's but a handful left. But the Church has always survived."

There's a handful of what?

Good Roman Catholic people. That will survive this period of the Church. Oh, this is what He said, "Right now, you can't be lukewarm, you can't be in between. You are either all Roman Catholic, or you're going to be a liberal."

You asked Him if the liberals will know that they're out of the Church?

My Father says they'll know. He said they're trying to bend things to suit their way of life.

1. Eileen George; with Cardinal Krol; being blessed by a priest before a service

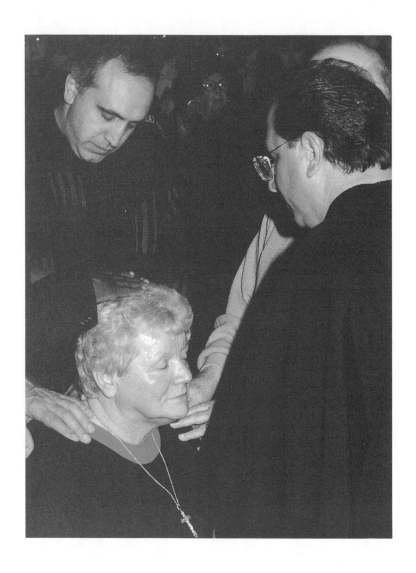

2. Priests praying over Eileen before a service

3. Eileen pointing out a healing

4. Franciscans in Assisi during a retreat given by Eileen to lay people

5. Eileen with her priest retreatants, Seoul, October 1993

6. Stephen Cardinal Kim celebrating the Mass preceding Eileen's service to more than 30,000 at the Olympic Gymnastic Stadium in Seoul, October 1993

7. Eileen in Korean dress

8. Eileen and her private chaplain, Fr. Augustine Esposito, OSA, with Mother Teresa's sisters to whom Eileen was giving a retreat

9. Eileen with Msgr. Anthony Wassel and (behind her) Father Eugene Wassel

10. Eileen feeding a pet lamb after a service

PART THREE: LOVING IS SERIOUS BUSINESS

11. THE CELEBRATION OF FATHER'S DAY
June 1983

I'd live here forever. It's not hot here, it's just right. The air is so still, yet it seems to be humming with peace. Even the flowers and the grass brushing against my face bring me peace. It's getting harder and harder to leave here, Butchie..... Sometimes I feel like I'm going through the motions of living, just existing.....

Yes, I do hear something. It's like music riding on the wind..... It's a chant and it's beautiful. If you wish..... I don't know from what direction. It seems like it's coming from all directions..... (laughs) I want to see and yet I want to stay here..... Well, help me up..... All right, You lead the way. It's beautiful, but it wasn't here before. Where did it come from?

(laughs) It's the Father, and He's celebrating. Look at Him. He sees us and He's asking us to come over. He's waving. Look at Him. Look how happy He looks Butchie. See how He's engulfed in the Spirit, He's radiant..... There's Michael. There's Mary. There's Thomasino and Doctor Mellifluous [St. Bernard]. They are all here.

Hi, my Father. What are you celebrating?..... I can't guess, Your birthday?..... **You don't have a birthday**..... (laughs) Of course I know. Father's day. Did You always do this, Father?..... **They do it for you.** I'm delighted. And look above, Father. They are sitting in jury boxes looking down upon us. I never saw them doing this before. What are they sitting in?..... Yes it's like a jury box, and yet it's not made of substance..... It's beautiful, Father. They are the choirs of angels. You're pretty special, Michael. You are right here with the Father.

Look at this. Who says they don't eat in Heaven? I'm sure some of Your priests do, Father. Let me see You drink it, Father. (laughs) See, You can drink and You can eat, and they say You're all spirit

[He is, in His Godhead]. (laughs)..... No, You have a nose and a mouth. For sure I'm delighted..... Well, thank You, but next to this, it's nothing. But I really wanted it to be something for You, Father..... I thank You.

I'm so happy You're pleased with me, Father. For real..... I think it's beautiful, I have never heard such beautiful music, such clear sharp voices..... And you too, Mother Mary, you look so beautiful and so radiant. You are in your rightful place, Mother..... Well, you helped me prepare for Him *[for Father's Day]*, Mother. That's why He likes me so much. 'Cause I asked your help. You're more beautiful than ever, my Mother.....

No, Father I'm not surprised at anything You do. Sometimes I may feel shocked. You're full of surprises. I know You like to party and You won't let this day go by, I'm sure. How I wish every one knew how You feel towards them, Father. How wonderful and happy You are. You like to be with people..... No, they think of You mostly as a judge, I guess, Father. But if they should look at the Daddy part of You, it would melt them away to nothing as it melts me, my Father..... I wish there was so much more I could have given to You, Father.....

(laughs) What a charming day. I'm so happy for You, Father. You deserve this and so much more, not just today, but every day, every minute, my Father..... For sure Mary knows that I love her. But I love You so much, Father. I want my whole life to be centered just on You. I get nervous when other things try to take me away from You..... I'm just delighted to be part of it.

And I'm happy to see you, Thomasino..... I'm happy to see you all. I get so spoiled when I'm here. I don't want to go home any more..... **This is my home.....** (laughs) Don't scold me, Thomasino..... Yes, I heard what He said. He said that He would put in a good word to the Father for me, and I could stay here. He was just teasing. He understands. They are all so beautiful and so happy with the Father. I wish every day could be a celebration like this with the Father.....

Look at His face, Thomasino, He's more beautiful than I have ever seen Him..... I know I'm very fortunate, and I love it when You call me "lass." I just love Him, and I know I'm blessed because He reveals Himself to me. And yet I suffer when I'm away from Him. I can't see Him all the time. So maybe in the blessing there's still a part of suffering. I know it's a blessing to see Him. A very unique and special blessing, and yet the price is loneliness afterwards, emptiness. I know He's there, but I want to be in His visible presence all the time.

Yes, my Father, You know it hurts me..... I understand..... There's so many of you here. I recognize many. I'm delighted that you let me take part..... You're very kind, Catherine. Yes, you do teach me much..... Yes, my Father, she does..... This is the most beautiful day I have ever had in my life. I just can't believe what's going on. And yet I see. Everything amazes me. The things I see upon this table. I know it's food, and yet I have never seen anything like it.....

The air is filled with happiness and sanctity. I can't describe it, my Father..... For sure I feel peace. Just the mysteries that are on this table alone would set us in awe, never mind anything else. (laughs) And that music, my Father, the heavenly choir..... Yes, I'm filled with peace. No, it's not just today, my Father, You bring me peace all the time but this is different..... They are dancing for You, Father. Look at their feet, it's as if they were ballet dancers, dancing on top of the blades of grass, not even crushing them. You delight in them, right, Father?..... It's just beautiful..... Together. Amazing. You sip from the goblet, and give it to me. My fingers go through it, and yet it is substance. It delights my soul. It's unlike anything I've ever tasted, my Father.....

I know you have, Father. You have filled my world with delight and many desirable things and pleasures, but nothing like this, Father..... (laughs) It reminds me of the marriage feast at Cana, You saved the best till last, but this last goes on forever, Father, ever and ever and ever. It seems as though I just came, and yet it seems as though I've been here for days and weeks. Not like a visitor, more like a belonger.....

Thank you, Michael. I feel as though I stand on familiar ground and yet my feet does not touch it..... I'm trying to recognize them all, my Father. Some faces are familiar and some I don't know..... They do? (laughs) They all know me..... I'm glad I'm one of them, Father.....

I've never heard You sing, Father, not like this..... It's very beautiful..... For me? (laughs) It's Your day, my Father, not mine..... If You wish..... I live to fulfill Your dreams, and hurry home to be with Thee, my Father. I like when You say it that way. Fulfill Your dreams and then hurry home to You, my Father..... That's a toast to overflowing..... It makes me feel sleepy.

INTERVIEW

He had quite a celebration, huh?
Yes. You hate to come back here.
There's so many who are there, all your friends and a lot of others?
Thomasino and Dr. Mellifluous, and Catherine, and Martin, Teresa, they were all there. And Michael.
And a lot that you didn't know?
A lot that I didn't know at all.
But they all knew you?
For sure they knew me. They all clapped when they saw me coming with Butchie to the Father.
They applauded, when you said you felt like you belong there?

Yes. Father's so beautiful, more today than ever. It's different there, it's different. All love, no jealousy, no fighting, no bickering, nothing but love. Everything so open and so honest.

And you were so accepted by everybody: They all knew you and loved you. The Father said you're one of them?

Yes. Mary looks so beautiful.

You said she was in her rightful place?

You know, they accept the love of Butchie for me. Catherine is His bride, yet no jealousy. It's different. They just want to help me to get there. To be one of them. There's no junk in between. And Butchie's never jealous of all the love my Father gives me. Nor are the people jealous of the love my Father gives me.

And the Father drank?

He drank.

What was it?

Delicious wine. (laughs)

And He gave you some too?

And the cup was like a goblet, neither gold nor silver. It was *[made of]* light. I could put my fingers through it, and yet I could drink from it and it was good. Isn't that beautiful?

Yes. And it wasn't hot there?

Nope, it wasn't hot, it wasn't cold, it was just nice, it was beautiful. Mary said, "It's a special gift of the Father allowing you to see us here." It's a very special gift. Once I went to my Father and I said, my Father how come I see You with bodies? I know I see You, my God, my Father. How come I see Thomasino with his body and all of them? These are special graces from my Father.

To see each one of them in their body?

Yes, because it's not their glorified body for sure. It's a body that He gives them until they have their glorified body. Thomasino said, "Don't think I'm keeping all of this," and he slapped his stomach. "Wait till you see me." (laughs) And I said, "Oh no, Thomas, don't change, I won't know you." "Oh yes you will," he said.

He calls you "lass," yes?

Yes, how do you know?

You said that he calls you "lass."

You listened again. Eavesdropper!

And so there was beautiful music too?

The music is something you have never heard.

You never heard the Father sing like that before?

This was different. Remember how I told you how He sang, and I said, "Father, who do you think you are, Bing Crosby?"

Doesn't He do that from time to time?

Yes, but not this way, this was a song and it was beautiful.

Oh, I see. He was singing a love song just for you?

Yes, just for me. Something about the wine.

What did He say?

I don't remember. It was about the wine. Something about "You drink the wine My lips have touched. To no child have I given so much." I can't remember it.

So they were all listening to Him sing?

Something about the wine was warm and sweet. It's like our souls, when we touch Him. I can't remember, but it was beautiful.

And He sang it like He was a professional singer?

(laughs) Sure He knows how to sing. It was simple and beautiful, so I could understand it.

And all the angels were there too?

Yes. Do you know how they were sitting? Like in a jury box. I remember once seeing an operation on television. People were surrounding it and looking down. These angels were all sitting up there, yet you couldn't see the beginning or the end of the box. And there was no end to the table, and yet you could see everyone.

Were people eating?

Yes, they were eating food, real stuff. I don't know what it was.

Did you eat it?

Nope, I only had the wine.

You never saw anything like it?

Never saw anything like it.

They were enjoying it?

Yes, they were happy people having a feast. Real happy people. We don't know what we're missing. (laughs) We're missing a lot. The Father loves us.

Well, what was it all about?

It was Father's Day.

He was so pleased with what you did for Him that He wanted you to join in the celebration?

He said, "I can count the gifts on one hand that the people have given the Father for Father's Day."

I said, "I'm glad I'm one of them, my Father." All He wants is a thought. He is so unselfish. A thought is like a million dollars to Him. Just the thought, "It's my Father God's Day."

And He was pleased because you asked Our Lady to help you give to Him?

Yes. She was helping me plan stuff and I said, "Mary, please tell me some words I can say to my Father to make Him happy and love me and be proud of me." But she would only say, "Eileen, He loves everything you say to Him. Write what you feel about the Father." She encouraged me.

To write a letter to Him?

For sure. I'm not saying anything. I know what your thinking. (laughs) "Well, I'm your director. Am I going to get these letters?" (laughs) Right?

It would be an act of humility to give your director the letter. It would be a double gift to the Father.

It would be an act of nosiness of my director. (laughs)

You said it was His day, not yours, what did He want to do?

Did He want to make it your day too?

Yes, He made everybody clap because I was there.

What about the love between you and Butchie. They could all see how much love there is between you?

For sure, and you know there's no jealousy.

How did you know that?

Catherine is His bride. Butchie brought me to the Father hugging me, and I looked up at Butchie and He kissed me in front of everybody. And He just loves me. Nobody is jealous. We're His brides. We're not jealous. Mary looks with so much love at the love between the Son and me. No jealousy.

You said, "You're in Your rightful place, Mother." Where was she?

She was at the table with the Father, right near Joseph.

The two of them were close to the Father and Butchie?

Right, right.

They were next to you and Butchie?

Michael was at the Father's right. And he just steps back a step when Butchie comes, and stays there right behind Butchie all the time.

And where are you, you're right beside Butchie?

Beside Butchie and then the Father took me right close to Him and put His arm around me.

And Mary and Joseph are next to Butchie?

No, they're not next to Butchie.

Where are they?

They are at the Father's left.

They are the closest to the Father on the left?

Yes. But Gabriel and Raphael are there. They step back, but they are there. They are always with my Father.

Did you ever see Butchie kiss or hug Catherine or His other brides?

Nope. I've never seen that. Even the Spirit was there and full of glow.

Around the Father?

Yep, around the Father.

Does the Spirit show you any special attention?

Oh yes. He always surrounds me with light when I go near Him. He's part of me. It feels like an infusion of love. It's hard to describe the Spirit's love, because He doesn't take a human form for me. But I know He's there and I know when I feel this infusion of love that He's loving me. Not like Butchie's loving, but He's loving me.

And you respond to that love, that surge of love?

For sure you do. It's hard to explain because He doesn't relate to me in a human form. He relates to me in love, and power, and light, and in different ways. But it's beautiful. See, the Father takes a form for me, and Butchie takes a form for me, and it's easy for me as a human to respond to Their love. But when the Spirit comes into me it's different.

You feel Him within you so that makes you respond?

Oh, for sure. It's beautiful.

12. LOVING YOU IS ALWAYS
   June 5, 1983

No, I don't think so. I am not distracted. I hear my name in the
wind, and I am afraid to answer. *[Her spiritual director is asking her
to speak.]* It will spoil my peace, and I don't want to be brought out
of this peace, Butchie. I am totally and completely relaxed in it.....
Yes, I meant it. I do find loving you a luxury. And it is a luxury that
I don't wish to share with others. I want it to be our time together.....
Selfish, maybe. Do you call it selfish for lovers not to want to be
disturbed, or invaded?..... Yes, I meant it. I think they make loving
You too complicated..... Well, sometimes I find You complicated.
But I never find Your love complicated, it's free flowing..... I just
feel peaceful about it..... Thank You.....

At times it makes me feel sad..... I don't know how to explain
it. I feel sad because You love us so and we take it for granted. It
doesn't even cut ice with us at times. And that makes me feel sad. I
felt sad at the prayer group because they were looking for extraor-
dinary things and they have Jesus right at their fingertips. I feel sad
about that, Butchie. I feel sad because they don't talk enough about
You and Your love, about the miracle of Your presence [in the
Blessed Sacrament.] Like they are chasing rainbows and the pot of
gold is right at their feet. I can't figure that one out, Butchie.....

(laughs) Maybe to an extent, I'm worried. I just can't understand..... We don't know what we're all about, I guess..... Maybe it
is a new infusion of love for You, but whatever it is, I like it, and it
is good..... (laughs) Thank You..... I just have an urge, a deep urge,
and I'm sure that it's from the Father, to make people know what
a luxury it is to love You. It's a deep craving at this moment, Butchie,
to make them understand, or try to make them understand what a
luxury it is to love You. And it is theirs just for the asking..... No, I
don't think so. I have always loved You, but it's somehow deeper

than that..... I don't know how deep. You'll have to ask the Father..... I told Him that they make You so complicated. He agrees..... I think instead of making loving You complicated, loving You uncomplicates everything. It makes everything freer.....

I'm sorry, Butchie, I can't agree with what they say. I don't like them pinning you down to structure. "I have to take my prayer time at this hour. I have to take my prayer time at that hour." Why don't they talk to You all the time? I think it's pretty good of them, giving you an hour. But I don't understand it, Butchie..... It's like they're trying to fit You into their schedule.

I don't mean to judge her. I love her dearly. You know I do, Butchie. It's like they're trying to fit you into a daily schedule, like washing the dishes or doing the floor. It has been bothering me all week. "This is my time for prayer. I give the Lord this time." That's really great that you give Him an hour or half an hour..... No, Butchie. I know You're glad to get that. But somehow, it doesn't sit right with me, Butchie. I don't know how You put up with us..... (laughs) I know You're content with a half an hour. But it's not right. It's been bugging me all week, Butchie..... No, not to a state of depression. I'm trying to figure out, what are we all about.....

It's as if I'm on the brink of something, and yet, in total darkness. I don't know if there is something the Father wants to tell me, Butchie. Tell the Spirit to make me open enough to grasp what He's saying..... I do talk to Him directly. I love Carsha.....

Carsha, help me with whatever my Father is trying to reveal to me about loving Butchie..... Of course I love Him. I want to love Him more..... There is something my Father is trying to tell me, Carsha, and I just can't seem to get it. Please help me..... **When two people are in love, as we should be in love with Jesus, you don't put the beloved in the closet and take him or her out when you're ready. You are always in union with the beloved. There is no set time, because you are so united. It is always a present thing,** togetherness. I understand, Carsha. I understand....

There is no set time to love Him. It is an ongoing thing. It is forever. It is always present, always there. By making a set time for the beloved, there is a finish and a beginning. This mustn't be in the love for Jesus. That is very beautiful, Carsha. That is so beautiful. I thank You. There is no set time to love Him. It is always.....
[Many find it helpful to have one or two set times daily for prayer. The bride comes from the nuptial chamber with an increased ardor of love, and does not stop loving the Beloved when the "set time" is over.]

I know, Carsha. That's the gift the Father gave me — the gift of "always." That is what He means. Always loving Him. Always present to Him. Carsha, I never connected these things. That's the gift of "always" and that's what we should seek. My Father gave me the gift of "always." That is so beautiful. It has no beginning and no end, it's "always." And that's how our love for Butchie should be. "Always." Don't tuck Him away in a closet, and pull Him out when you are ready to give Him a half hour. Generous souls that we are..... "Always."

So we must seek the gift of "always," Carsha. See how much I need You. See how much I love You, Carsha. I can't survive without You..... I know You love me. The gift of "always." That's what I must get through to my people, my priests. The gift of "always." And cut free from being structured. Now it's time to eat. Now it's time to sleep. Now it's time to be with the Lord. Seek ye the gift of "always." Be ever so present, ever so ready. Let there be no beginning to thy love, no end. It will be for always. Your life will change, for you will exist in Him and He in you for always. That is very beautiful, Carsha. Thank You so much.....

Carsha, my soul is weeping for joy. I need You so badly. I need You because You're so smart and You have such wisdom. And I'm nothing..... Sure, it's not only my eyes that weep, Carsha. My soul weeps with joy and gratefulness and love. Oh, Carsha, I truly love

You. The gift of "always."

Father, I never quite understood this gift, and yet, I thought I did. The gift of "always," Father. All week my head has been pounding and wondering why we think we give so generously. A half an hour to Butchie. An hour. Like we're feeding a beggar. And it has bothered me so much, my Father..... Yes, Father, even to hear it from so-called charismatic people. The structure bothered me, and the thought of us being so generous kept stabbing at my soul, Father. I couldn't quite handle it or know how to deal with it......

I think I do now, my Father. I know I do. There is no set time for loving You. It is permanent. It is always. No beginning. No end. This is what the gift of "always" is, Father..... I understand it more clearly. It is beautiful, Father. I must give it to the priests and the people. "Always. Always." Don't stick our Love in the closet and pull Him out when we feel generous. Forever love Him. Always. Always present. There is no time. Father, I love the gifts that You give me. And I love the way You space the time, to get me into a deeper knowledge of these gifts. I don't think I could cope with [receiving] all of it [at once]. Thanks to Carsha, I understand..... Yes, it does touch me deeply, Father. I told Carsha not only my eyes cry, but my soul is crying with joy, with love.

So much I want to give Your people, Father. I want them to love You as I love You. I want them to love Butchie as I love Him. I want them to get rid of all this surface junk..... It began this week, Father. Every day they would call me, "I'm giving Him an hour of my time today." It made me feel like, big deal! You give the Savior an hour of your time. Yet, I know Butchie is so glad to get that hour. He's so filled with love for us. It broke my heart all week, Father. I couldn't understand why I was being so bugged by this.....

I must give it to them, Father. And Carsha will help me, won't you, Carsha..... I thank You, Father, for all the love that You put in my heart for Carsha. A love beyond all understanding. Your Holy

Spirit..... I'm deeply touched, Father. I'm so moved because it is a new awakening to Your love, Butchie's love and Carsha's love..... I know. The gifts they seek are wrong [and wrongly sought.] Not to the point of loving You, but to the point of being filled with glory and vanity, projecting not the gifts of the Spirit, but themselves. Father, if I ever do this, knock me down and step on me. Bury me deep into the ground, so I will never be filled with vanity or pride..... Let me use Your gifts, my Father, to bring glory to you, not that You need it. I would bring souls to thee, Father.....

How can I tell them there is so much more, my Father?..... I don't think it's sadness, Father. I just think I'm overwhelmed..... You agree? Thank You, Father..... **I must bring the tenderness and the love of their God unto the Roman Catholic Church. I must never waiver.....** Yes, my Father..... No, I delight in it because I know when I speak, Father, it's Carsha who speaks through me to Your people..... Thank You, Father..... Yes, I know I have learned much today..... **The secret of holiness.....** I know that, Father. **To me, much has been given, and much will be asked.** But You will help me, won't You, Father?..... Nope. I'm not afraid..... I love You too, my Father. I'm just so overwhelmed with the gift of "always." So overwhelmed..... **I will light up the dark corners of the Church. Where there is darkness I will bring light. And where there is sadness I will bring joy. Where there is no faith, I will kindle the flame. And where there is hatred, I will bring love.....** It seems like quite a mission, Father..... No..... Thank You, Father..... Whatever You say. Whatever You say, Father.....

13. LIFE IS NOT ALL PEACHES AND CREAM
June 5, 1983

I always find peace here. It seems as though I just can't bring my troubles here, Butchie..... Maybe it's because I find so much peace, I don't want to return, and yet, I know I have work to do..... No, it's not a burden. It's just that I know it's something I have to do..... Day by day it gets harder to leave here..... Of course it does. You know all things. You know I'm hurting..... No, they don't understand..... No, I don't think it's too much. I can still take a lot..... My Father knows. If I could hide it from Him, I would.

Sometimes I rejoice that He knows it, and other times I don't want to burden Him with it, Butchie..... I don't think even the doctor knows because he can't seem to put his finger on anything..... I just can't explain it. This morning it was so painful, it hurt so bad, I had to do everything so I wouldn't cry. Even when I tried to rest the pain was so bad, Butchie. I don't want to talk about it now. I can't understand it..... Nope, I'm not sad over it. Well, listen, I don't enjoy it, I'll tell you. But I've found that I can use it while I have it and it seems like I always have it..... No, it doesn't make me sad. It hurts an awful lot. I don't think anybody knows how much it hurts but You and the Father..... I used that one for the priests. It's really bad when it wakes me out of a sleep, right? So that goes for the priests, Butchie..... I'd rather talk about something else.....

I just don't know how this world functions. I know it's led by the Spirit. I'd rather talk about the beauty that's here..... There's light, but there's no sun..... I don't mean to change the subject. I don't think I could because you know the pain is there. My Father knows it. So we know it. Do we have to talk about it? Let's talk about here..... I'm wondering where all this light comes from when there's no sun..... **From the Spirit......** Well what if somebody wanted sun..... **You give them everything they love.** Would You put a sun there for them if they loved the sun?..... And I love the rain. Will You give me rain at times?..... The rain has a purpose. Here you don't need rain. It'll be raining for my enjoyment, to make me happy. But the flowers don't need it to drink. Nor is rain needed to fill the brooks and the streams. It will be given to make me happy. I think that's neat.....

How come You don't tell all these secrets to everybody? They'd like to know them, you know..... If I tell them, they're going to label me as a cuckoo nut or a dodo bird, or as flaky. So I think if You tell them..... (laughs) If they're not open to Your regular graces, they're not going to be open to this..... Poor Butchie, You have an awful job on Your hands with us. I bet You thought it was going to end on the cross. You didn't realize You had all this work to do with us until the end of time..... You did.....

I don't know. Why are You asking me such a silly question?..... I'm thinking about it, but I think it's silly. Why do I love You so much?..... I can't say it's because You died for me. I wouldn't want anyone I love to die for me. I think because we grew up together, and You're always with me. I love You more and more each time. Why are You asking me such a silly question? How do I know why I love You so much? I just love You..... Nope, I can't attribute it to the cross. I think it's a neat thing You did. I don't know how You could do it, but I wouldn't ask anybody I love to die on the cross. I just love You because, I guess because You are love itself. Does that make sense?.....

(laughs) I think we should switch it around. Why do You love me? I'm so dumb and so stupid, so icky. I disappoint You in many things. I try to be good, and fail You in so many things. How do You like the shoe on that foot, hey?..... I don't know about that, Butch, but if I can't run to You and the Father, who am I going to run to? I'd be in awful trouble all the time..... I don't know. I think when You hide on me, I realize more than ever how much I need

You. Sometimes I take You for granted. You're always around, and yet, I love You. But when You hide on me and I have to find You and pursue You, I realize how much I miss You and how much I need You. Maybe that's the time I love You most..... For sure I do. That's why I go to communion. I love You because You're close and You're comforting me, but somehow I realize it more when I'm in pursuit of You. I just ache all over. I feel alone and I ache all over and I know I have to be with You or I will die.....

For sure I love You to kiss and to hold me and hug me and to love me, but then I've got You. It's when I haven't got You, then I go searching for You..... It's a pain of loss, of emptiness. If You want to get me here fast, hide on me, and I'll have a heart attack and I'll be here fast. You better watch it and don't hide unless You know what You're in for..... (laughs) Call it what You like.....

Don't get back to my sickness. I don't want to talk about it..... No, nobody knows how much pain I have..... I said something to him *[her director]* but he doesn't know it..... Nope. They *[her family]* don't know it. I think because I function. But sometimes it is so bad, Butchie, I think I'm going to lose my mind. I can't do things it's so bad..... See, You made me talk about it, and I don't want to talk about it. You aren't going to make me lose the merit, are You, Butch?..... **I'm not losing merit when I talk to You about it.....** But I want to bring You happiness, I don't want to bring You sadness. You know it's there, and that's it..... (laughs) You are funny..... Well, You can do anything You want after I'm gone. That's Your business. But now I think You have to listen to me, at least for a little bit, right?..... I mean seeing You're asking..... (laughs) They're beautiful. Where'd You sneak those from? I didn't see You pick them.....

You do? With the Father?..... (laughs) **You discuss all of this with the Father.....** No. I don't want them to know this. You can do what You want when I'm not here. That's Your business. But I wish You wouldn't let anybody know it now. I have enough troubles doing what I'm doing..... (laughs) I'll be all right. They are joys, for sure..... Well, I do offer it for the mission..... I think I'm right in keeping it quiet, Butchie. Catherine taught me that. It's like I have a secret with the Father..... With You, Butchie, too, and with the Spirit. And people don't know. They're always telling me how fine I look and how great things are and I'm so wonderful. But I'm so happy to have a secret. It makes me feel, "You don't know everything.".....

(laughs) Catherine said there is more merit in keeping it quiet, so we're going to keep it quiet, right?..... I don't care if they never know it. The Father knows it and You know it. That's all that matters to me..... (laughs) That's what You think. If they only knew it's not peaches and cream. If they only knew what goes on behind the scenes..... You're saying **not by prayer alone. By sacrifice and suffering.....**

You can open *[doors, services]* as many as you want. You'll give me the graces, I'm sure..... (laughs) I can laugh at it now, but I don't think I can laugh when it happens *[sufferings imposed by others].....* I use my humanness as a cop-out, Butchie, but I don't know. I think it's my pride, Butch..... Of course I can love them. Although I'd like to belt them and love them later..... Well, if You get angry I guess I can too, a little..... That's up to the Father..... (laughs) Yes, I knew He was listening.....

Butchie said when I'm gone You'll reveal how much I hurt and how much I suffer..... (laughs) That's up to You. I can't stop You now and I won't be able to stop You then..... Of course I love You, Father..... Yes, it does hurt a lot, Father. I don't understand it. I claim it's the weather. Sometimes it hurts so bad..... The hip, yes. It goes down to the knee..... Well, You understand it, Father. If I could hide it from You, I would, but You know everything..... You've opened many doors, Father..... I'll come whenever You wish.

INTERVIEW

Was Butchie asking you why you love Him so much?

I guess.

Which answer did He like best?

I don't know. He laughed when I said it's not because He died on the cross for me. I told Him I think I love Him the most when He's gone. That's when I understand that I love Him the most.

When you tell Him that, you're asking for trouble.

I know. He'll hide on me, I bet. I hope not.

You realize your love for Him more keenly when He's not around?

When He's not around. And then I miss Him so much. You know you never realize until you lose something. And then you say, Oh my gosh! I never realized He was such a part of me, so much. I knew it, but now that He's gone I understand it more. I'm in pursuit of Him constantly.

So when the Father came you really relaxed, didn't you?

My Father? For sure. You know what I was just thinking? My Father, how He smells all the time so beautiful. It's like fresh air. Butchie's robes always smell like sheets blowing in the breeze. And my Father always has such an aroma about Him. It draws you to Him. It's something different. It's not a perfumy smell. It's holiness I guess. It's just so clean and so perfect you could eat Him up. (laughs).

What happened at the end when you were so silent?

My Father? He was hugging me, kissing me and loving me. I love to feel the warmth of His cheek. When He touches you, your cheek, it goes right down to your very toes. It's just so different. You know you're loved. He doesn't have to say any-thing, you just know it, and you feel all that trust in His love, all that fullness in it. There's no doubt about it, you're loved.

And protected.

You feel protected. Everything at once. He just takes His little finger and rubs it up and down your face like He does often. There's so much in that. It's security. It's everything. Everything is in that love. And His look, it seems to touch the depths of your very soul. You can't feel your soul, yet you know His look is touching it. They belong together. It's hard to explain. Just the way He looks penetrates into your soul. You can't touch your soul, but you know it's being touched. (laughs). Do you understand what I'm saying? It's just beautiful. I'm crazy about the Father. I wish sometimes I could hide things from Him because I only want to bring Him happiness.

He didn't explain what was causing you all the suffering?

My Father? I hurt so bad at times. I can't explain it. But He called me today when I was in such pain I couldn't eat. The pain is like an untouchable.

It's in your knee?

It's in my feet. It's in my hip. I just can't explain it. The other day it was like a sharp sword pushing into me when I tried to lift my foot to get into the van. It was real bad. Well anyway, it doesn't matter. My Father is using it.

He said it was helping priests?

For sure. It doesn't matter and it's a good secret between my Father and me. Everybody is always saying, You're the picture of health. I do look the picture of health.

But didn't He say that after you come to Him He's going to let them know that it wasn't all peaches and cream?

Yes. Right. He said, "Little do they know what is going on within you, Eileen. They don't have to know right now. It's between you and the Father." They think everything is OK. She has gifts. She's a gifted lady. They think everything is filled with glory.

14. LOVING IS SERIOUS STUFF
August 7, 1983

I don't want to walk right now, I just want to sit here and be quiet. It's so peaceful..... It seems like the trees are whispering, Butchie, and the birds are telling each other we're here..... Yes, I do feel more relaxed..... It's just that I need quiet so badly. It's almost a year of noise and confusion *[Since the fire destroyed their home in September 1982, Eileen and her family have been living in a small trailer]*. It's like it's way out of reach, and I can't have it any more..... I just feel all wound up like an alarm clock, and like my springs are going to give..... Yes, like I'd be scattered all over..... I guess it's a little bit of everything. I don't think it's all the house. I think that the dogs have a lot to do with it, and the aggravation of people coming all the time. They mean well..... How can I tell them? I just can't. They mean well.....

I hope so, Butchie. I hope so..... **If it lasts.** Why do You say that? .....**You don't think it will last.** Maybe it's because the time is getting so close to being in my own house *[which is being built on the site of her destroyed house]*. Maybe it's Capi. Maybe it's myself. I just don't want to hear all this stuff anymore *[from the people who call her]*..... No, some new ones, but it seems as though they're always the old ones, with new aches and pains and troubles. Almost like they thrive on it, Butchie..... I don't mean to judge them.....

At times I feel like I'm backsliding, Butchie. Only here do I feel as though I've got it all together. I feel like I'm backsliding when I can't get to Mass. I feel like I'm not pleasing You..... **It could come from him also.** Oh sure, I would go to Mass if I could..... **And he's trying to make me feel bad about it.....** Yes. I know I would if I could..... **Then I shouldn't feel bad about it?** But I feel like I'm backsliding..... I feel as though I'm not advancing at all, Butchie. I've never felt this bad about it before. Look how long it is in between

Masses..... He's using a good thing to floor me..... I'm listening..... As long as my intentions are there, and I would if I could. These circumstances have changed it. I'm letting him pull me down, and he's using a perfectly good thing to clobber me.....

But I still feel as though I'm backsliding, Butchie. You know the clanging cymbal? I feel as though all the voices are clanging in my ear. I don't want to hear half that stuff. I pray for them, but I don't want to hear all this junk. I know each one thinks they're the only one. How would You handle it, Butchie, so they won't get their feathers ruffled or be upset with me?..... I remember that. They listened for awhile.....

No, I don't think I'm sad over it, Butchie. I think I'm just so wound up that I'm going to give, pop, like the springs of the clock, and be shattered all over the place..... **You will pick me up.** Then You want me to pop?..... **You don't want me to pop.....** Then You better tell them not to call me..... I know they're hurting, Butchie, but I hear the same things over and over and it's usually the same people. They get out of one situation and they're in another. Like they thrive on it..... Of course I love it here in the valley..... Nope, at this point I'd come right now, even with the house as it is. I would like to settle it for the children, but I feel at my wits end.....

Don't do that. Don't do that, Butchie..... No, I'm not mad. You know I'm not mad. I just don't think You're paying attention to what I'm saying. Don't do that..... Listen. Listen. Butchie, listen to me! I want my peace back..... I don't mean to let them invade here, but I'm trying to have You help me out of this situation..... Am I really bringing them here? I don't mean to, Butchie..... Well that's how it is when I'm back at the trailer and back in the house. They're either on the phone or in the house or they're in my thoughts. I don't want them there..... **As long as I pray for them.....**

I want to do tapes and I want to be with my Father, and I want You to speak to me more often, Butchie, and I want to go on the

walks we used to go on..... Maybe because it's so close to the end.....
You're God, take care of it. What can I do but pray?..... I feel like
You gave me a tranquilizer and I want to go to sleep here and forget everything..... But I used to feel this peace in my own home. It
was just You and I and the Father..... Of course, Carsha, too. But I
don't think it's too far out that I can't get it any more.....

Of course I love the Father..... Yes. I know He loves me..... Yes,
I believe I have work to do..... Of course I believe Carsha will help
me..... He said I would ride a bright stallion of faith..... Right..... He
said I would be used in the reform and in this revolution in the
Church. What can I do? I can't even handle my every day situa-
tions and He wants me to reform the Church. You've got to be
kidding, Butchie..... Nope, I don't underestimate Him, for sure,
but I think He got His marbles mixed up when He chose me to do
this. I can't even straighten out my own life..... I felt it, Butchie,
with all my heart, and I felt as though they knew there was a revolution in the Church. I picked it up from them..... **The hour of
decision is here. Either we're going to be or we're not going to
be.....** That sounds important..... With all my heart, I love You.....

Butchie, I don't want mushy stuff. I want to talk about serious
stuff..... You're being silly. Let's talk about serious stuff, all right?.....
Well, about the revolution in the Church..... Does the holy Father
know this?..... He does? And what is he doing about it?..... Yes, I
heard about that..... Well, they call him many things. The medieval Pope..... Of course not. The Father is telling me..... I do when
Carsha inspires me to do it..... Tell me the best way to prepare.....
(laughs) You are cuckoo today. Butchie, I love You with all my
heart, but I want to talk about serious stuff. Why do You keep going
backwards with me when I'm really serious?..... My serious face? I
mean business..... Yep. See, that's my serious face..... (laughs) You
are silly..... Anyway, what are we going to do to help the Father?.....
I'm happy about that, as long as Carsha does His part..... I'm hap-

py about that too. (laughs) You're silly. I love You more than ever..... I'm showing You by doing my Father's work.....

Father, He's a cuckoo nut. He is so mushy. I'm trying to talk about serious stuff..... Well, about the revolution in the Church, Father..... (laughs) You tell Him, Father..... **Loving Him is serious stuff.** See, Father says this is serious stuff, Butchie..... (laughs) **When I'm loving Butchie I'm really doing serious things in the Church, because in this loving, I reflect the Father and His love to His people.....** You're on His side, right?..... (laughs) **Nobody's side, and yet, both of our sides.....** Whatever You wish..... I really do think it could get worse, but I don't want to upset You by talking about it.....

Maybe Butchie has the right idea of loving and finding peace in each other, and praying, but not worrying so much..... Yes, I see it His way. I can see the heavy burden upon You, Father, and when You're loving me, and Butchie's loving me, I see nothing but peace and joy in You, and that's where I want You to be, my Father. I don't want You to worry about all this stuff. And I shouldn't even bring it up except to let You know I'm ready to do anything You want, my Father..... I will go through any door You wish..... For sure I present it to him *[her director]* first. You always tell me to do this, Father.....

You act as though there is going to be a thick time..... Then why did you say You'll stand by me through thick or thin? (laughs) You act as though there is something coming, Father..... There is so much peace here, Father. I breathe better. I feel better. I need this peace, Father. The only thing is, I don't want to go back..... I told Butchie I feel like a clock all wound up tight and those springs are ready to pop. But here I find peace in my Father's love and my Butchie's love and the warmth and the love of my Spirit.....

Yes, Father, the house is almost done. A lot of odds and ends. Then I will have my peace..... **I must be firm.....** How can I be firm,

Father?..... **Tell them to stay away.....** I couldn't do that..... **In a nice way.....** Will they understand it, Father?..... **With the mighty mission ahead of me, I need peace, silence and solitude where I can respond to my Father's words and His love.....** I understand that..... **Where I can hear His commands and fulfill them and no foreign bodies will seep in and distract me from the road my Father is calling me to.....** Then help me get this silence and solitude and peace that I need, my Father..... **In spite of them, through the light of the Holy Spirit, I must respect this peace that I seek.....** For sure I want to function in Your light and Your love..... **It's very essential that I get this peace.....** See, You're back to serious stuff with me. I was trying to take You from it..... I'm not afraid of anything You want me to do, my Father. I have Butchie and I have You and Carsha..... I have Mother Mary with me. And Michael, and Raphael, and all the saints. I'm not afraid of anything.

Father, talking about the saints, Father, asked me a question. Why do You let Thomasino come with his big pot belly, and why do You let them have bodies when they're not supposed to have bodies until they have a glorified body? Father wants to know..... Nope, I don't care. I just take it the way it comes, but You should answer the question, I think..... **Because with their glorified bodies, I would not be able to stand the rays of light that comes from them.....** All right. Wait a minute now. Back up, my Father. Then how come I can stand the light from Butchie and from You and from Mary?..... All right, then, won't their light be guided and directed by the Holy Spirit, Father?..... Oh. **Then if You didn't let them come this way, I could never respond to them because they wouldn't have their glorified bodies and I wouldn't know who they were and I couldn't build up a relationship with them.** How am I going to explain all this stuff to him? I'll forget it.....

I understand what You want me to know. But I don't think he'll understand what I'm going to say. You allow me to see them as they truly were, Thomasino and Catherine and Martin and Doctor Mellifluous. Right? So I will know who they are. You're the Father and You can do anything You want. If they were in their glorified bodies, which they can't be now, then I couldn't identify with them..... No, I think that's pretty cool..... I'm comfortable with what You do. I'm not digging into anything.....

You can send me anybody You want. I love them all. He's the one that fires the questions at me. I'm just happy with what You're doing. I'm just content, Father. Anything You do is OK by me. He's the brain that wants to know all this stuff. Anything You do is OK by me. You always have such neat arrangements.....

(laughs) I love You too, Father. I love You so much, I want the whole world to love You as I love You. Not quite as much because I want to love You the best. I don't want anyone to love You as much as I love You. I just want to love You more than everybody, but I want them to love You..... How much?..... I don't know. But not quite as much as me. I'm supposed to love You the best. Not more than You, Butchie, but I'm supposed to love Him the best as a human, and I don't want anybody to love You as much as I do, but I want them to love You. Does that sound awful?..... (laughs) **It sounds neat.** You're catching all my slang, Father. They won't know You're God if You keep talking like I do. You'll lose Your identity..... Thank You, Father..... Whatever and whenever, I'll be ready..... (laughs) He's Your mushy Son. Like Father, like Son.

INTERVIEW

You brought my question about the bodies to the Father.
Oh yes. It's a miracle I remembered to ask Him.
Yes. What did He explain to you.
He said, "First of all, Eileen, I'm the Father. I'm God. I can do anything I want." He said, "Could you identify Thomasino with a

glorified body, instead of the way He looks now?" I said, "No, I guess not." He said, "Eileen, first of all, they're not ready for their glorified bodies. Second, I have to give them their regular forms so you'll understand who they are and who you're working with."

What do you mean their regular forms? The way they looked when they were alive?

On earth. Thomasino is just as rolly-polly as he was. And he loves it. He keeps saying, "Don't think this is going to be my glorified body. I'm going to look slick." And the Father said that's how I identify with them. And He said, "If they had their glorified bodies, your eyes wouldn't be able to behold them." And I said, "Well, Father, I can see You." And He said, "That's because the Spirit is protecting you from the light of the Father and the Son. If they had their glorified bodies, number one, you wouldn't recognize them. Number two, you couldn't bear to look at them. Number three, you couldn't have the relationship you have with them." Is it clearer now? Do you understand why He lets me see them in their bodies in the valley, Thomasino and Doctor Mellifluous and everybody else ?

You said to the Father that I wanted to know all this stuff. What did He say?

He said, "Well, Eileen, you can't blame him for wanting to know." I said, "But I take everything for granted, Father. You put Thomasino and Doctor Mellifluous and Catherine there." He said, "But Eileen, you see them. Father doesn't see what you see and so he wants an explanation about what is going on." I said, "Well, OK. If You want me to tell him. I understand what You're saying, but I don't know if he'll understand." He said, "Eileen, he'll have the grace. He'll understand."

Good. I'd like to know what happened when you told your Father that if He uses your vocabulary, He's going to lose His identity.

(laughing) He laughed. He said, "Let me worry about that, Child. Let me worry about that."

And then you said, "Thank You, Father."

He said, "Do you know how much I love you?" And I said, Thank You, Father.

Well, then what happened when you said, "Mushy Son like Father."

Butchie came over and gave me a big kiss and hug and squeeze. He got His nose in it again. I said, "Like Father, like Son. Mushy. Mushy. Mushy." My Father laughed.

The Father was kissing you?

He hugged me and kissed me too.

And Butchie wanted to come and do the same?

Yes. He wants more loving. He was lovable today.

He was loving today?

More than usual.

And the Father explained that that's serious business when He's loving you.

That's right, because He's teaching me to fall into a deeper union with Him and my Father and the Spirit, and then I reflect this to my people. Sometimes loving is a lot more teaching, my Father said, then the actual teaching itself. Because when I'm loving Him, I'm growing in a deeper union with Butchie, and my people pick up the love that I have. At my service Sunday, they came to me downstairs and they said, "Oh you truly know He's there. We can tell it by the way you look and the way you talk about Jesus." I got that through loving Him, not through teachings. Sometimes loving is more.

So the world could be better converted by more loving?

By more loving.

You're very frustrated and ready to explode. Its been going on for a year with all the people, the telephone, the dogs, the trailer, and so on.

I feel like a wound up alarm clock ready to pop its springs.

Did the Father and Butchie have any ideas about that?.....

Yes, they told me to stay in silence and solitude. And they said, "No matter how painful it's going to be for you, tell these people you love them, but you're not socializing with anyone." He told me the same thing before. "Eileen, you give your best at your talks and your conferences. They're to leave you alone, because your silence and solitude and your love with Butchie and the Father and the Spirit prepares you for your next talk, and in Their love you find the power to speak." And if I don't have the quietness to love, then I'm not going to have the power to speak to them.

Are you going to be able to tell them that?

I'll be able to tell them.

Will they understand?

They will.

Will they leave you alone then?

No, they're going to keep bugging me for awhile, but then they'll get the message.

So you're going to carry that out?

I hope so, with my Father's grace. If I don't, something's going to happen.

What's going to happen?

My springs will pop. I'll be scattered. Nothing will make an alarm clock tick unless it's all put together. And if I scatter, then nothing is going to work. You know, if I have an explosion.

He said if you had an explosion He'd put you together again.

He'll put me together if I stay in silence and solitude. Loving Butchie and being in the presence of my Father prepares me from service to service. But I shouldn't bring them to the valley by talking about them.

You mean when you come to the valley, you talk about them?

I talked about them today. He chastised me with love. He said, "Eileen, you're bringing them into this valley. There is no place for them here." So He didn't want me to talk about them in my valley.

You must have talked about them when you said how frustrated you were.

Yes. He said that I was bringing them in, but that's just an example. "After they talk to you, you think about what they said, so they're taking two spaces of your time." He's very happy if I do my best at a talk. I socialize with them downstairs *[at St. John's Church after her fourth Sunday of the month service]* and then they're not to bother me after that.

When you asked him how He would handle it so as not to get their feathers ruffled and so they would not be upset with you, that's what He explained?

Right.

And you asked Him to prevent them from calling you?

I told Him to do it, but He doesn't tamper with the will.

The Father was telling you about the revolution in the Church and the reform of the Church. What was He talking about?

He was talking about the revolution and the uprising in the Church. He talked about the naughty things they said about the Holy Father. And He said, "This is nothing but revolution, Eileen, and the Church refuses to face it. But I'm sending you on your white charger of faith and you're going to change this." I said, "Me?" He said, "Yes, you. It'll be the work of Carsha doing it through you."

And you said, Father, how can I do that, you've got your marbles mixed. How can I do that when I can't even straighten out my own situation. So what did He say to that?

He said, "You'll do it. With the power of the Spirit."

He said, " It's the hour of decision. Either we're going to be or not be."

(laughing) I told Him He sounded like a poet. To be or not to be, that is the question. And He started laughing and then He went like this. *[She puts her thumbs on her chest under her jacket.]* Like He was Napoleon. He's got a good sense of humor, the Father, but He can be strict. He can be tough.

And you asked Him if the Holy Father knows what is going on. And He must of said that he does.

He said he does.

And you asked, "What is he doing about it?"

He's doing everything he can about it. But they're calling him the medieval Pope. They're saying he's outdated. And the Catholic papers are publishing this. They shouldn't be printing that stuff in their papers. I don't care whether it's being liberal or not. They're not supposed to do that. They're supposed to defend him. He's not putting the Church backwards. He's not setting us back on our heels. He's just making us toe the mark of what we should be. The liberals put it in a different light. But he doesn't do this.

You said to the Father, "Tell me the best way to prepare."

My Father said the best way for me to prepare for my mission here on earth is to be alone with the Father, the Son, and the Holy Spirit. And He included Mary. I should run to her. But He said, "The best way to prepare is to love the Father, the Son and the Holy Spirit. Let them be a part of your life and live in their presence." That would prepare me for anything I have to talk about, any mission whatsoever that He places before me. So if you live in His presence, you're prepared for everything. Right?

Yes, that's right.

Oh, there's one thing Butchie said. I felt I was backsliding today because I haven't been able to go to Mass. I can't leave the dogs, they'll tear the place apart. And He said, "Eileen, I don't want confusion. I know you would get there if you could." He said, "You've never missed Mass before. And there's a reason for it."

He said, "Don't let the evil one put you on a guilt trip. This isn't good what he's trying to do to you." I feel bad. He's making me feel like I'm backsliding.

So you're not backsliding?

Butchie says I'm not.

If you could get to Mass, you would.

He knows I would. Even if I had to walk. I'd get there.

So the Father is pleased.

Of course He is. He said, "You're not backsliding. That back-sliding idea comes from Capi. See, he does a job on you, under the pretense of a good angel."

Then He spoke about the doors that He was going to open and He said he'd stand by you through thick and thin. Who?

The Father. He said, "It's not going to be easy when I open doors for you to go through and to preach My word. But remember, I'll stand by you through thick and thin." He also said that you would stand by me.

And then He said, "You must be firm." That's with the people? You said, "How can I be firm?" And He said, "Tell them to stay away." I'm getting to that point now.

15. THE BANNER OF TRUTH
August 14, 1983

I know, but sometimes my tiredness seems to leave me when I'm here. I'm sure when I go back I will be tired again. But I'm not tired right now. I feel light and easy. Almost like I could fly, Butchie..... No, I find rest here. I do try to live up to that [moderation in working], but sometimes I get carried away. There's so much to do..... My Father would just ask me how I did today. He won't ask me about all those things I have to do..... Oh, sure, it's easy for you to say, "I'll wake up and it'll all be there"..... Well, I do worry about what people say..... **I shouldn't worry about what they say, just what the Father says. One day at a time.....**

How come You don't feel the wear and tear of everything? You have more to do than I and You always look so young and so spiffy. Don't You ever get tired?..... Oh, **You got tired in Your humanness, but now You don't.....** Yes, that must be why the Father has so much patience with us, He doesn't tire. I lose patience with the kids. I get tired of saying things over and over, but look how many times the Father has to say them. Don't do that with that grass. I'm talking serious stuff, Butchie..... When I'm serious I have to look serious, right?.....

I'm listening to everything You're saying. I know You're right, You're the Father's Kid, but I don't agree with You sometimes, even though You're right.....

I see water. Butchie, don't keep doing that with the grass. It makes me twitch. Are You doing it to aggravate me?..... (laughs) If that's love, then don't love me so much with it..... I see grass and I see water and the water looks tasty, clear, crystal-like. Everything is so beautiful.

The water sounds melodious coming over those rocks, like it's singing to You..... Yes, it does bring me peace, Butchie. See, You know how to bring me peace. The sound of the water bubbling over the rocks brings me peace..... Flowers? Yes they bring peace..... **When I start to get upset think of the stream and the flowers.** I'll be thinking of them all the time because I'm always upset..... Do I really have shackles tying me down?..... Well I don't think I'm a slave to the house, Butchie. I want to get it in order. Don't You want it to look good?..... **Up to the point of my tiredness.** You want me to slow down?..... For sure I will..... **Always the stream flows gently. The flowers sway in the breeze gently, not with hard labor.....** No. I just want to sit here and rest my head on Your shoulder. I don't want to talk about all that stuff. I'm really tired.....

You can ask me anything You want, if I know the answer..... You are saying I'm more tired than usual..... I think it's because I'm lacking in sleep..... Yes, it hurts at times..... Are they truly signs?..... Nope I'm not afraid.....

It's so peaceful here, so unspoiled. I just hate to go back, Butchie. I talk about Father X running. I feel like I'm running all the time..... **He's running from God and I'm running to God.....** But isn't he in search of the Father?..... **He would have found Him in his parish.** Then why didn't You tell him so? Am I running as much as he?..... Well, isn't running to the Father good?..... **Not to a point of fatigue. Father doesn't want His children to be tired and worn out. They should advance gently in a graceful manner, slowly but securely......**

Nope, I could just fall asleep here at any time, I don't want to go back and start that turmoil over again. I get lost in this peace. I yearn for it so much. I am so happy to help these souls, like the sisters, but I don't want to go back there, Butchie. Isn't that awful?..... I know I helped them a lot. They were so grateful, and they are yearning for a deeper love for the Father. I feel like I'm a terrible person. I just want to be left alone with You, like I am here in the valley. I want to be in my home with You. I don't want these people around. I love them, You know that I love them, but I'm just so tired of them. A whole year of them, day after day, after day. I can't do anything else any more except pray..... Yes, I do feel very relaxed, very joyful, very peaceful. I don't want them invading our life. But how can I stop it?..... If You say so. It looks beautiful, just beautiful..... Thank You. How do I feel? Refreshed..... No, You bring me peace.

I'm relaxing with Butchie, Father..... Yes, I have been tired..... I don't mean to be a concern to You, Father. I just know what has to be done and I guess I'm the only one who will do it. I don't mind doing it, I just get tired..... Don't say that, Father. **If I get too tired, I won't be able to be of service to You.** How can I stop from being tired, Father?..... Those are just the people that are draining me. I feel as though my family is draining me. I know I should be doing it, Father..... I do tell them, Father. It goes in one ear and out the other. They have so many other things to do, I guess..... Nope, I don't want to block what I'm supposed to be doing for You..... **If I keep doing this, I'll be too tired to speak or to hear Your word.....** I know You made me a human..... Right, **I can only take so much. And if I wear myself out like this, then I can't be of service to my Father. I'll be too tired.** What shall I do Father?.....

You can make things a lot easier. Send down all Your helpers and let them do my work..... Well, what about Martin, he folded clothes for me..... I don't think it's so silly, I think it's just being logical. You don't want me to wear myself out in chores that have to be done. Because You want me to preach Your word. Then why don't You send somebody down to help me?..... Well, inspire them.....

I'm listening. **It's going to be a very powerful meeting at La-Salette. But I must rest so I can be at my best for You, Father.** What do You mean by powerful?..... **The Spirit will flow freely.....** What are we going to talk about and who's going to be there.....

(laughs) Well, at least I try to get a hint, right?..... **There will be priests.** How many, Father?..... **Many.** How many is many?..... **A few.** How many is a few? You're just playing games with me, you monkey..... I love You too, Father..... I know, Father, but I promise I'll go easy. Because I do want to be alert to the Spirit and to reveal everything the Spirit wishes revealed to His people.....

You really think it will be, Father? If You say so, I believe You..... (laughs) **I'll hit them like a storm.** A good storm or a bad one?..... **Good.** Good. Will You be proud of me?..... That makes me feel good. It gives me new life..... Oh, **You will proclaim "That's my daughter."** That's beautiful. Why won't You let them hear it? (laughs)..... Then we'll take them by storm..... I will? Would You care to reveal his name, Father?..... Nope, that's OK, it's not important. As long as he's touched..... Don't worry about my health. You're in full control and I'll be all right. I promise to take a rest every day. I know I promised You before. I'll leave everything, Father. Because I do want to do what You want me to do. And I want to work in Carsha's light..... Yes, my Father.....

You really do? **You feel like crying when I'm tired.** Well I won't be tired any more, so don't cry. I'll take it easy and I'll take my nap. I don't want You to cry over something like that, Father..... Yes, yes..... Nope, I'm listening to everything You're saying. I'm not dozing off. I'm absorbing it. I just like to keep my head here and hug You so tight. *[Eileen loves to kneel before the Father with her head in His lap, hugging His knees].* I know why I don't let You go any more. I just love to hear those nice things You say. And I get lost in them. I can't believe You're talking to me.....

Oh, I tell You a hundred times I love You more than anybody in the whole world. You're my Dad and I adore You from the depths of my very soul. You have the cutest chubby cheeks and the sweetest nose and the prettiest eyes I have ever seen. And I just love You to pieces, Daddy..... No, when You look at me I know that I truly belong and that I'm loved. And all my tiredness leaves me, Father. It's like I'm a new creation.....

Yes. I don't care how much work there will be. I know I won't be tired. You'll give me the grace to do it..... I will ride a stallion of faith..... Right, it's a revolution in the Church. And I will bring them a banner of truth: Doctrine and Tradition..... I'll be on a mighty charger. And it will be the wisdom of His Spirit..... What will these arrows mean, my Father? Will they pierce me, will I fall?..... They will wound me but I will not fall. There will be victory. The Son, the power of the Spirit and the Father will triumph over everything and everyone. And I'll be such a part of that. Father, that thrills me to death, to life.....

No, no. Don't weep when I'm tired, I won't be tired any more. I will rest..... My illness. Oh I know it's there. It's like an untouchable. I can't see it, I can't feel it, and yet I know it's there boring away at me, Father. I know I'm not free from it, although many think I am, including my mother, Father. But I know it's there. It's like an animal waiting for its prey. I'm not afraid. I'm alert, but I know it's there like a raging wolf ready to devour me. And yet I'm not afraid of it. I know it's little right now, but I also know that it will be set free soon, Father. But I'll be strong because You will make me strong..... No, there's no time to waste. We must do it together. Right? (laughs)..... Free as a bird..... I know my days are numbered, as You say. We'll do it, Father, don't You worry, we'll do it together..... Yes, I want to please You in everything. It's You and I against the whole world and we're going to make it..... Right, and You're not going to grieve any more because I'm tired. I don't want You to weep over silly stuff like that. I'm going to rest and we're going to do everything You want us to do.....

It is? My tiredness is feeding my sickness. How can it feed my sickness, Father? I believe You, but I'd like to know..... Depression and weakness. I understand but I'm not going to let that happen.

Right? (laughs)..... I love You too. I love You so much. Did You like the way the nuns started to love You, Father?..... I'm glad You're delighted. And they're going to love You more because they are beginning to know You more..... I did tell them that..... Thank You, Father..... Yes, I'll remember. No more tears. Right?.... I promise.....

INTERVIEW

Well, the Father had an explanation of how you could fight this tiredness?

The Father said the tiredness that I feel or that I allow to take over feeds my illness. And He says that He has work for me to do, and that when He sees me so tired, He actually weeps. And then I can't function, and He knows that, and He says so does the devil. So He told me that I have to get rest every afternoon. He said, "Even if you don't feel like it." He says the devil is very happy when I'm tired, because it's starting to feed the illness. And depression, frustration and anxiety can come in, and this makes the illness spread fast. Then He said, "Up until now I've been trying to keep you from it. It seems like you're falling into it further. But, Eileen, don't let it happen because I weep over this."

But how can you prevent it from happening?

He wants me to cut free from these people, 'cause they are draining me. W called the first thing this morning, she drains me, and V called. I didn't take her call. I get upset because she has no money. She is always looking for money.

It was good that you didn't take her call.

Well, they didn't give it to me. They told me after she hung up. My Father said, "This is the medicine that makes the cancer spread faster." I have to get away from it. He said that I have a powerful work to do. This revolution is taking place in the Church.

And He says that Carsha will be there to help me. I ache because I'm working so much. It never dawned on me that this is a tool of the devil. The devil can use my illness to depress me, to fill me with frustration and anxiety. Then I can't function. The Father said it's going to be a powerful meeting at LaSalette. He said I'm going to touch more than a few priests there.

Good. How about those sisters you spoke to?

He said they were deeply touched, and they're starting to renew themselves in the Father's love. He said what amazes them is that I'm a family person and not a religious. It puts them to shame. But that's a good quality — they know what's right, so that's good.

Did He tell you how you could . . . ?

He said pretty soon my house will be done and I can cut free from all the calls. He said to start now. Teach them what is right.

You have to explain that to your family so they will cooperate.

I told Joan. She was so hurt. I said, "Joan, I love you dearly but I am not used to taking all these calls from somebody." She called me Friday and I said, "Listen, honey, I love you, and I pray for you, but I don't take these calls because they take me away from my family."

You pray for her?

Yes, yes.

That's the best you can do, isn't it?

I felt really bad about it. But I had to do it. He said, "Be gracious and kind, and if they truly love you, they'll understand."

How about the rest He wants you to take, how can you get that?

I'll have to get off my feet after lunch, He says, regardless. That's a time to put aside for rest.

And if they are visiting?

Just break away from them. My Father says I can't get through to some of these people. But if I pray and they are open, maybe grace can get through to them. He said I deeply touched Sister. She cried. The Father said that she was deeply moved and she will be a different person, seeking a deeper union with God.

The Father wants you to slow down in your work in the house?

He said, "If you die tonight, Eileen, and you come to Me, I'll only judge you on what you did, not what you were going to do tomorrow." He said, "Just one day at a time, remember that. It's essential."

So that means that you don't have to work at night to make headway with the washing?

Yes, yes. He wants us to move gently and slowly.

Did He explain that to you?

Yes He did. He said, "Just do today's work. Tomorrow's work will be there. But if I call you tonight, I'm going to say you did today's work. I'm not going to ask you if you went into tomorrow's work. So take one day at a time, and go at a slower pace with it." I feel as though I have a limited time. I'm trying to make sure everybody has the right clothes and everything.

You'll have more time to set up the house if you don't aggravate the illness.

The house is set up pretty well now, except for curtains. The cellar isn't set up. There's a lot to do down there. But it is really remarkable how the upstairs took shape. (laughs) Butchie's always right, He's never wrong. It's so awful to be dealing with a guy who's never wrong.

Butchie did something in your love time, and you asked Him not to. He was using some grass?

He was tickling my nose. He knows I don't like it.

And, so He explained it by saying that He's loving you?

Yes.

And you said, you didn't want Him to love you so much.

(laughs) Isn't that awful. He takes long pieces of grass and He tickles under my nose. He knows that it gives me goose pimples. And He does it all the time. And sometimes He takes His hand and runs it through my hair. He's very loving. I don't mind that.

Did He tell you that when you're upset to think of the flowers?

He told me when I was upset to think of the brook in my valley. It was flowing ever so gently. It actually gave me peace to see it flowing over the little rocks, praising the Savior, almost showing off. How gently it flowed, not rushing, ever so gentle. Then He asked me to look at the flowers. They were swaying in the breeze, back and forth, very gently to the left, to the right. Not working, just moving gently and gracefully. He said, "When you get frustrated, Eileen, think of this stream and its gentleness, and think of those flowers near the stream and their gentleness, and you'll calm down right away." They do calm me, just looking at them. That's a beautiful thought.

Yes, that's beautiful. So that would help you and then you'd move more slowly and gracefully too?

Right.

He doesn't want you to be a slave to your house.

No. I'm up and down those stairs a hundred and ten times an hour. Back and forth, back and forth, it's a lot you know.

You haven't got the physical strength you think you have.

No. I told my Father today, I can feel the cancer in me. I can't touch it, I can't see it, and yet I know it's there. It's like a sleeping dog.

It prevents you from having the strength you used to have?

I know it's taking my strength away without my realizing it. I sat down with Earl the other night, and I said, "Dad, remember you used to go to work and come home and you never knew where your bedroom was going to be?" I would move the bedroom from one room to the other, bureaus and beds. Take them down and put them up myself and change the curtains all in one day. And I said, "I can't even move a chair now. I just have no strength."

Of course you would have if it weren't for the cancer.

Of course I would. I know it's there. I know there's something wacky with my system.

And what did He say about the early signs?

Oh, there are signs that the cancer is progressing, and it doesn't show itself yet. But He said, "You know it is moving, Eileen. You're not afraid?" I said, "No, I'm not afraid." I'm certainly not afraid of the cancer. People tell me — my own mother tells me — I'm healed. I know I am not healed. I can feel it within me. Sometimes I feel it in my perspiration.

It's good that you feel it because if you think that you're well, you'll overdo it.

I know that. I was so tired I just wanted to crawl in bed and say the heck with everything. I'm going to die. I'm not going to get up to eat. I'm tired of fighting.

That's the depression.

You don't know how much I'm hurting in different areas, physically. My Father knows this. I ache and I'm sore and I struggle and people will come and say, "Gee, you look great." (laughs)

Your head started to go down, Eileen and you said, "I'm not dozing off, I'm listening to every . . . "

Oh, I was just snuggling up to His knees. He said, "Are you going to sleep?" His words are like soothing ointment. You're lulled into a peace but not a sleep. He said He had work for me to do.

He wants you to be free as a bird?

Right. I can't have any attachment. The telephone is an attachment. These people coming into my house are an attachment.

Your housework is an attachment?

Right, it's an attachment. I have to be free in order to do my Father's work. He said, "I have work for you to do." I will ride the white stallion of faith. I must bring people back to the true doctrine and tradition of the Roman Catholic Church. We have gotten away from it. He said that they were going to throw arrows at me. And I asked my Father if I'd be wounded. He said "You'll be wounded but you won't fall. You will still go on teaching the true doctrine and tradition of the Roman Catholic Church." He probably means I'm going to be hurt.

He explained that before, "The wounds won't get to your heart." You will be wounded but your heart won't be affected.

He emphasizes so much that they can't get to me.

Because your heart will be in love with Butchie and with Him.

Right. He emphasizes so much the true doctrine and tradition of the Church. He's always after the liberals. He doesn't like the liberals. He said to me today, "If they're liberal they are lukewarm and I will vomit them from my mouth."

He said before that they were like your dog that was dying and couldn't do anything to help itself and you had to carry it?

He said the priest was a liberal and he was like my dog that was dying. But when he dies he's going to bring himself to perdition. Other liberal priests are out preaching liberal doctrine, but this priest isn't preaching it. They are bringing many souls to perdition and this is very bad stuff. You can't let the liberal stuff win. My Father has been emphasizing true doctrine and tradition for a long time.

How about the conservatives, does He ever talk about them?

The traditionalist are out because they broke with the Pope.

But what about the conservatives?

I never asked Him about them. What do you mean "conservatives"?

They don't want changes.

No, see that won't do either, because if the Pope makes changes we have to be subject to authority. Remember He said there was never a disobedient saint and there never will be. My Father told me not to receive Communion in the hand. It's optional. But if the Pope says every Catholic has to receive Communion in the hand, I certainly would receive Communion in my hand. My Father wants me to be subject to authority. My obedience will be to the Pope and the Pope has to give an account to God why he made that rule. See, I have the easy side of it, all I have to do is obey. I'll say, Father, he told me to do it. (laughs)

16. THREE AGAINST ONE
End of August, or beginning of September, 1983

I know I do. I find peace with them *[the dogs]*. I sit in the cellar and they jump in my lap. You really love them, don't you, Butchie?..... **Because they bring me happiness.....** Thank you, Butchie, that makes me feel good.....

Nope, it's not bothering me talking about it. I'm relaxing. You can talk about it. I'll listen to you..... Yes I saw You in the middle aisle..... I'm glad, Butchie, I'm glad You're pleased and the Father is pleased. I was glad I was so open to the Spirit. But it's wonderful to come here and relax. I tried so many times to relax in my room..... The only time I did was when Thomasino came in. He had so much to say. There is always somebody knocking at the door or listening at the door *[during her retreats]*. I don't know what they want to hear..... Yeah, I guess they do invade my privacy. I know they don't mean to, but I'm being smothered. And I want peace. I want an escape.....

Of course I'm happy if You're happy and the Father's happy. The Holy Spirit did a fine job. I really prayed to Him, Butchie. I would never go to a service without His novena. I know where my strength comes from, Butchie.....

I remember when the Bishop said with all this power and love, that I still am myself, there's no change in me. Maybe it's because You make me understand what I am, Butchie. I know I'm great before You. You love me and I'm Your bride. But I know also that I'm not capable of anything at all except through the Spirit. I never forget that and I don't want to forget it. And I could never forget it. I know that's the truth.....

I'm glad he does, Butchie. I admire all those beautiful things in him. He's a fine Bishop. You love him, huh, Butchie?.....

I know You don't like the way they flock around me. I don't

like it either, Butchie. They make me feel like something I'm not. It's not through my efforts, it's through Your Spirit's efforts. Carsha sticks ever so close to me.....

Many door will open. Do You want me to go through them, Butchie?..... **First give them to my spiritual director.....** Right..... Nope it's easy for me to do that.....

They love me up there on the podium, You love me right here..... Your happy with me, Butchie?..... (laughs) Thank you. As long as You're happy..... First You tell me the Father is going to open a lot of doors, now You ask me if I want to come here forever. Butchie, You're confusing me. How can I come here forever if the Father is going to open the doors? You're just tempting me.

(laughs) Father, You're listening! Butchie said You're going to open many doors in New York for me, and then He says — look at Him. He's laughing 'cause I'm squealing. (laughs) Then He asked me if I want to come here. Now You're getting the eye from the Father, Butchie..... Father, give Him Your eye. (laughs) We're both giving You the eye, Butchie..... **Two against one.** (laughs) **Three.** (laughs) Even Carsha's against You. (laughing) How do You give the eye, Carsha? (laughs) That's it, Butchie..... Yes. See Carsha has power..... Father, He's really silly..... Does He really want me here, my Father?..... That much He wants me here? But He wants me to do Your will, right?..... Right. **He knows that if I say but the word You'll take me.** (laughs) Easy way to make me say it. He'll give You the eye, Butchie.

I'm glad You were proud of me, Father. I was proud of the way You allowed the Spirit to work through me, Father..... I love him too, Father, he's a real good Bishop and I'm glad he loves me. I'm very happy that he says that I'm unspoiled. Are You happy about that, Father?..... That's why You don't want me to lose my identity? 'Cause in it I'm unspoiled? What do You mean by unspoiled, Father?..... The Bishop said because I don't think I'm a big shot. I'm just an ordinary person and he says that I'm filled with love.

Do You think I'm filled with love, my Father? I wish I were filled with more love, Father..... I don't know what makes me think I haven't got enough. I think because of judging..... Well, where's the line between judging and discerning? If I was filled with love would I overlook it?..... **That would be a fault.** I don't want to be filled with that kind of love then. I know I have enough faults. I don't want more faults. I just want to be filled with the right kind of love..... **Right love is discerning regardless of how it hurts. There has to be discernment.**

What about the anger that filled my heart when X said it was a good meeting and she knew they all talked, my Father? I was judging..... **I wasn't judging. Because three of them called and said that it was disrespectful, irreverent.** Then how do I take care of that, Father? One minute she listens and one minute she doesn't. I don't know what to do, Father. Carsha will have to help me in this. They ask advice. When I give it to them they don't follow it, Father. Not that it's my advice, my Father, I know it's the Spirit's advice. By myself I would give them the wrong advice, but I know the Spirit's not wrong, Father.....

Who would want to cash in on a nothing, Father? When I get back home that's when I get my identity back. I wash my pans, hang up clothes. "Where's my shirt?", that's my identity. Who could cash in on me, I'm a nothing. I don't even take money for myself. How could they cash in on me?.....

(sneezes) I'm allergic to You. (laughs)..... Don't do that. You can do it if You want, Father..... There, that makes it feel better. I feel it clearing right into my very lungs. Thank you, Father.....

(laughs) No, we'll talk..... That's what Butchie says. **Many doors will be open to me.** What ever You wish, my Father..... My director, **I'll tell him first, for sure.....** You know him Father, he loves the Bishop. He loves all priests who walk straight, my Father.....

All I want to do is to be a credit to You, Father. It's great being up there and talking to them and it's wonderful seeing a full house, but the most important thing is to know You're with me, Father. To know that Butchie's there and Carsha's there. That's the most important thing to me..... Thank you, Father.....

You do have great things planned for me?..... I'm excited. Sure I'm excited, as long as You plan them for me, Father. And I know I'll have Carsha's help..... **That's why I need the silence and solitude before and after to prepare for my Father's work.** Again You say that, Father.....

I don't mind *[unjust criticism]*. It hurts me for a minute but it doesn't bother me..... I do think of it, Father. But I'm human. You know I'm human and You wouldn't want me to be indifferent to it. Of course it hurts for a while and then if I think of it I might get a little upset. But You've been so good about that, my Father, You help me forget these things..... I know, but don't feel bad about it. You know what I am, my Father. Don't let those things bother You, Father. You tell me to rise above it. You're God, how are You going to rise? Don't dwell on it, Father. I love You with all my heart.

If they did that to Butchie, what will they do to me — make mince meat out of me? So what. They can't touch my soul, You said, Father. We are not going to worry about that, Father, are we? Don't feel sad about it. We don't care, Father. It will make us more powerful and it will bring more souls to You, Father..... (laughs) Yes..... For sure I do love You..... I am listening, Father. **I will shine as the beacon light before all men. And I will bring my Father's word to them. It is not by chance that I am here or there, but by the Father's will. A new light has been sent to God's people and it will light up the whole world.....** That's wonderful Father, but I hope I don't let You down. I wouldn't want to let You down, Father.....

INTERVIEW

He said, "Why don't you stay here with Me." I told my Father and I said, "Father give Him the eye." The Father and I stared at Butchie and He made believe that He couldn't stand it. (laughs)

What about Carsha, you told Carsha to give Him the eye?

He knocked Him on His rump. (laughs) A ray came Zoomm. (laughs) Butchie laughed His head off. He's so nutty. So nutty, Butchie.

That was a powerful ray?

(laughs) He really knocked Him down. Zoomm. That was His eye. (laughs) Right on His back. (laughs) Butchie just laughed His head off. It didn't bother Him. They really love One Another. They really love. Isn't it funny?

They play with each other too, huh?

For sure, it's beautiful, just beautiful. We've made everything so black and white, yes and no. As if God had no enjoyment and no love. They call it love but it's a coldness. They don't realize how much love the Father truly is and how He loves to laugh and be part of our lives. It's too bad we miss so much. And how the Spirit just delights in Butchie and They kid each other and They laugh. We miss everything. We make Church so straight laced. You can be straight laced but you have to realize there is so much love in that Family of God and we're missing so much. I don't know if we'll ever get it. (laughs) Butchie was laughing and laughing and you could just feel the delight in the Spirit for doing it. And the Father was laughing.

And Butchie was in the air?

He's on His back but He's not touching the ground. Just laughing so much, They love each other. They enjoy each other. We make everything so cut and dry. We're missing so much. I gave Butchie the eye and the Father did too.

The same as you?

Yep, we both had our mouths open giving Him the eye and I said, " Spirit, You do it too." And the Spirit went Zoomm. The Father roared. And Butchie didn't get mad. He laughed.

Well, He knows all the love that's there.

Of course. There's so much love. They play. They play games.

What other games have you seen Them play?

Once I saw Butchie reaching for His wine at the table and it was in a goblet of beautiful light, but its a goblet, and I saw the Father moving it. He said, "Watch this," and moved it. The Father kept moving the goblet. The Father was laughing. And Butchie knew only the Father could do that. And Butchie said, "All right, Father." (laughs) Isn't that funny? They play all kinds of games. It's beautiful. Once when Butchie asked me to go behind the tree, when we got there the Father removed the tree. (laughs)

Was the Father there when Butchie said come behind the tree?

Yeah, I saw Him but Butchie was in front. Butchie said, "Eileen, there was a tree here. Go over behind that one." He looked at me and He's laughing. That tree was gone, too. (laughs) The Father was playing games with Him. Butchie said, "All right, Father. You'll have Your time, leave Eileen and Me alone." (laughs) But so much love. Nobody gets mad, it's beautiful, it's just beautiful. Nobody gets angry and nobody gets jealous. That's all. Good bye.

NOTE. *Eileen loves innocent pranks. The Father enters into this spirit. He takes delight in amusing Eileen, as do Jesus and the Holy Spirit. This provides a counterpoint to the seriousness of their conversations. When Eileen gets very serious, both the Father and Jesus distract her momentarily. One of the ways They do this is by showing Their affection for her. They wish to make her realize that the most important thing in her life and her mission is to grow in love.*

PART FOUR: A REVOLUTION OF LOVE

17. WHAT THE FATHER WANTS HIS PEOPLE TO KNOW
September 21, 1983

[Eileen is repeating what Jesus is saying while coughing] That cough makes moisture come from my body. I was exerting the cough, because within my throat there is a tickle, and it's still there. (coughs) The love of my Butchie lies within my heart. It tickles my tongue with excitement, and I spit out words that act as moisture to other souls. And they don't wipe it away, they let it absorb into their very flesh, their very soul. And they are nourished by these words that come through Eileen from the Spirit. I absorb Jesus. His love tickles not my throat but my tongue, so that I can't hold back His love, and I spit — that sounds pretty vulgar, Butchie, "spit"!..... They understand vulgarity. All right. And I spit out — that sounds awful. Butchie, You're going to have to give me another word..... All right, I'll do that — His love. And then they absorb the moisture that was in my heart and it saturates them in body and soul.

I get the message!..... I certainly do. I feel it. It's like a tear I shed by exerting myself. And they cry tears of joy for this new awakening to their God. That's very beautiful, Butchie. But did You have to make my throat hurt and tickle it to give me a teaching?..... You didn't do it. I'll remember that teaching well..... The moisture must spread through the whole congregation. Isn't that the work of the Spirit, Butchie? Doesn't He have to open the doors, so they'll be open and accept the grace?.....

Are they really moving that fast, Butchie? They are like a cancer, destroying the Church. I know You won't tamper with the free will, but couldn't You kind of trip them up, at least slow them down a little?.....

Father, he *[her director]* keeps asking me what You want published. I don't know except what You tell me. I know You want the revelations about the Mass, and how just one Mass heard properly could save the whole world. That blows my mind, Father. Look how many I have heard. I'm in trouble..... I know, but You're always making allowances for me. I'm afraid of a cop-out..... If You make the allowances I'm willing to go along with You.....

You want me to tell him about the Mass. What else, my Father?..... About the revelations of the Eucharist, especially the ones from Thomasino. I can't remember them all. They keep coming. I will jot them down, Father. **And You want me to tell him about the Sacrament of Reconciliation.** What else, Father?..... **I must tell him about the angels, and the choirs of angels. And the three choirs that You have revealed to me that man knows nothing about. Their functions and duties, and the duties of Michael, Raphael, Gabriel and the guardian angels.** I think the world's kind of messed up on that, Father. They think the guardian angels are supposed to save us when we get hit by a car or fall off a cliff. They don't know the real duties of the angels, Father, to guard us in our spiritual life. There's so much. I could do a whole book on that myself, my Father..... Right. **I should not hold back.**

The different plateaus of Heaven, and what exists on these plateaus. What Heaven is all about, and what we will do. The people there are completely happy..... **The true duties of a priest and the dignity of the priest. The dignity of the bishops and the shepherds. The revelations of priesthood and sisterhood.** Oh, there is so much, my Father, so much. I don't know when I am going to get all this done.....

You want them to know about the gift of the Rosary. The true gift of Mary to Your people. I don't know how I'm going to do that one. I know You'll give me the way and the right words.....

There is so much You want to tell Your people..... Thomasino?..... Right, **the angels. Not only their different functions but also their different languages.** Why would all this interest them?.....

Some it would, and some might not understand it, but those who will understand are the ones who will benefit by it. The theologians will know that I get my words from the Father. But will they accept it, Father?..... They don't like having a halter on, Father. They want to be free..... Well, they are not obedient. Nobody's obeying anybody. My pastor said that a year ago..... I will be very unpopular, Father..... Who cares? We don't care, right?..... (laughs) You are looking through me. I guess I do care sometimes. I hate to see somebody fighting me.....

I'll do everything I can, Father..... Right. I'll put it down as I remember it, and I'll give it to him..... The world will receive revelations like they have never received, far greater than at the time of my friend Thomasino. Thomasino was helping my mind to open the doors to the knowledge of the Father. Because he is teaching me about the angels and the saints like a Philadelphia lawyer!.....

You are pretty great, Father. I'll listen closely to Thomasino, and I will write and I will keep these notes and give them to my director, Father..... I understand. He is excited about it?..... (laughs) I will enkindle in the hearts of Your people a fire of burning love, and it will be the everlasting torch. It will burn on and on. And it will be ignited from one person to the other. That's great, Father. Just as You said cancer is spreading throughout the Church, this fire of love for the Father and for the kingdom will spread.....

There is so much You want to tell them, Father. I would need a thousand books..... I'll be open to anything You want..... About Heaven. Its beauty and everything about it. You know, Father, being a place where you have to be good all the time, I think these earthlings think they are going to get bored. Nothing to do but walk around and pray. They don't understand. It's a beautiful, magnificent place, untouched by sin. Everything is alive and vibrant. This is what we must tell them. They'll eat, they'll enjoy, they'll be merry. A perfect place, no heartaches, no sorrow, no regrets.

They don't think you can eat in Heaven. I know they are think-ing of eating to survive, not to enjoy. I had that run-in this week. "The dogs can't get into Heaven." And I told Sister what You said, Father, that they get there not because they have merited it, but because I have merited it and I love them. So You give them to me. They don't look at You as a kind, wonderful Father. They look at You as a judge who's out to get them.....

(laughs) **We'll both get them.** Imagine! They don't think you ever eat in Heaven. Everything we ever enjoyed outside of sin is ours. They don't understand You at all, Father..... I'll tell them about the plateaus and the flowers and the brooks and how everything bows to its Creator. And the love and the aroma and the presence of the Father......

See, this holy expectation of Heaven and being there forever, this fire must be enkindled in the hearts of God's children. The joy that He'll be coming one day to claim them, not sorrow be-cause they think it's over. Joy because it is just beginning, begin-ning to live, not just exist.....

I know You love me. There's no doubt whatever in my mind, It appeases my very soul, my heart. There is no other feeling like it and yet I know there is so much more. And that is what I must tell them. **The many veils between the Father and His children and how love lets the veils fall away and draws us closer to Him.** They don't understand that, Father. They think if they are going to see You, they are going to drop dead!

(laughs) I think it's silly too. But they have to understand what it is all about, my Father. All I can do is tell it as I see it. Is that good enough for You?.....

18. MAKING THE PEOPLE HUNGER FOR THEIR GOD
September 28, 1983

You know how much I love being here. There is no other place like it, Butchie..... I know. I know that the Father has work for us to do..... Yes, You, the Father, the Spirit. All of us, Butchie..... But who wouldn't want to stay here forever? They don't know it, that's why they don't crave it. But once they had seen it, they would long for it and never be content any other place.....

What are You looking at? That's my ring..... For sure. I never forget it's there for a moment, Butchie..... I know. It means the same thing to me, Butchie. Maybe not as much as to You; I don't fully understand it..... (laughs) Did He really say that? "She wears my ring." But the whole world doesn't see it. You're the only one that sees it..... (laughs) I know that You love me. And I love You too, Butchie. With all my heart, I love You.....

I'm very happy that You're proud of me..... Yes. It's just that sometimes You distract me. I can't take my eyes off of You. And people say they know that I see something..... (laughs) Of course I see something, I see You. You are so funny!.....

You really feel like that? (laughs) I wonder what they'd say if they heard You saying that out loud so that they could all hear..... Butchie, You are really silly today!..... (laughs) For sure I do. You make me feel like Peter..... Well, I'm glad You want me here badly. I want to be here also, but my Father has work for me to do, and You said Yourself, that You want me to do the Father's work..... (laughs) Is that for sure? **You never come to the valley when I'm not here.....** You are funny.....

Nope. I delight in it. I am very happy about that. I don't know if I could take any more revelations, Butchie. I have so many to sort out in my brain right now..... Bilocation, trilocation, sure. I understand them both..... You mean here I can be in two places at once? What is the purpose of that, Butchie?..... (laughs) **Love isn't purpose enough.** For You it is..... Whatever You say. That means I could be here in my valley, and I could be in another place at the same time?..... Would that be a contradiction?..... (laughs) No? **A gift.** I understand. I think that is super..... Well, yes, I think that's quite a revelation. (laughs) **I can bilocate here.** I think that's great. And I like the purpose even better. (laughs)..... You are full of surprises, for sure.

Tell me some more..... For sure?..... I like that part of it. That is beautiful. Like I would be the only person there?..... I'm not going to ask You how You'll do it. I believe You for sure. That's wonderful..... Now I know. But, when I can go to two places at once, that's for us. Is it for all the brides of Christ?..... (laughs) Am I one of the specials?..... You are funny. You are so funny..... I love You dearly. Sometimes I love You so much that I think my heart's going to blow open. And sometimes I love the Father as if it were going to blow my mind.....

Tell me some more, Love. I know You can't tell it to me all at once, but tell me some more..... **There is a very special place that You and I go together. And I can go there without leaving my valley.....** Nope. I think that's super. Just like we go special places now..... Butchie, there are so many things You reveal to me. I don't know if the people would understand them..... **All is possible in the kingdom. Nothing is impossible. There is no such word in the kingdom as "impossible." All is positive, no negative.....** (laughs) I'm looking forward to it, for sure..... You're so loving today, Butchie. You're always loving, but twice as sweet today..... Well, maybe so. But You do have those special, tender moments..... I'm glad. I hope my Father is just as proud of me.....

(laughs) I knew You were listening..... Thank You, Father..... Butchie is revealing more and more to me about the kingdom, my Father. I take it You want people to know about Your kingdom, my Father..... But if there's no reason they shouldn't, then why don't You tell them, instead of me telling them all this stuff?..... **You speak through vessels.** Am I a vessel, my Father?..... **Priceless.** (laughs) I don't know. "Vessel, " I agree with You..... If You say so..... **A vessel of grace.** I like that name. I'm a vessel of grace. I'm a vessel, and I'm carrying Your grace to the people. (laughs) **Your graces..... Your wisdom. Your knowledge. Your revelations.** What about Your love, Father?..... (laughs) That's very important..... That's very beautiful. For sure it is.....

Have I really stirred them all? The whole diocese is stirred? (laughs) That's what You wanted, right, Father?..... Yes, there were quite a few priests. Was that what You wanted, Father?..... Sure, then I'm happy. I'm just delighted..... **I must tell them everything about Your kingdom.** I don't know everything, Father. But You're doing pretty good with some of this stuff. You just told me some stuff that I didn't know..... They just think it's one big, dull place. Everybody is a goody two shoe, and they're all going to get bored. They don't know the fascinating corners. Behind every nook and cranny, there is something beautiful, something magnificent to see and to feel, to expect, to have. There is just so much more.....

I try to. I really try, my Father..... Sunday? Were they really in awe, Father?..... **That's because I gave away some of my secrets.** (laughs)..... It's all right to do that, my Father?..... The Spirit did, for sure, because I wouldn't tell them that ordinarily.....

(laughs) I knew that You were listening, Holy Spirit..... (laughs) For sure..... I was delighted that You brought it to my mind, Carsha. I truly was..... The ones who came to me were in awe. They never realized that it was so beautiful. They just put it in a category: Heaven or Hell, come or go. They were just so excited about Heaven. So I guess You're right, Holy Spirit. **It's time to reveal this stuff to them, to excite them about the kingdom, about the angels.....**

Yes, Butchie, about You too. **In the Eucharist.** I could never forget that. They don't know what they're missing..... The angels were?..... Well I saw Michael and Raphael and Gabriel and Hosches. That's about it. That's all the Father revealed to me.

Father, why didn't You reveal the rest of the gang to me?..... Were they excited, Carsha? I'm so happy..... That's what I'm all about..... Well, You reveal to me whatever You want me to tell them and I will tell them..... You look so pleased, my Father..... That's what You say..... (laughs) I don't know about the whole diocese, but if You say it, Father. I believe what You say..... The priests, they are truly being stirred, my Father?..... That's what You want?..... Great. I'm glad. For sure I am..... You look so happy, Father, and Your eyes are sparkling so beautifully. And not with tears, either. Just pure happiness. That's the way I always want to picture You, Father. I don't want You to have any heavy weights from us.....

You are so beautiful, Father. Just so handsome and so beautiful. Everything is in Your face, my Father..... (laughs) You want me to tell You more?..... You are silly. I'm not telling You anything else because You'll get pompous..... (laughs) You are funny..... Well, You told me two minutes ago, but You can tell me again. I love to hear it..... Thank You, Father. Now tell me some more about what You want me to do..... **Feed Father everything You teach me.....** (laughs) With a spoon?..... You are funny..... Sometimes I forget, my Father. (laughs) I have it taped but I forget to use it..... See, my mind is weak..... **We are going to whet the appetites of Your people. We're not going to tell them everything. But we're going to tell them enough to make them hunger and thirst for their God, to make them hunger and thirst for the kingdom of Heaven so they won't want to be shackled to the earth by worldly goods or sinful deeds.....** I'm all for that, Father..... I'll reveal to him whatever You reveal to me.....

I hope. I just can't remember sometimes, so You'll have to help me in that area, Father..... You will give me a list, and I will have to write it..... I must tell him that everybody has an angel. It's not myth or fiction. It's truth. And what the angels do, and what they don't do. And what Michael does and the things that he does not do..... I will, Father..... And Raphael and Gabriel. Not only the guardian angels. I will tell them about the different choirs of angels, and the language of the angels. That no man knows the language of the angels. And I will reveal to him what Thomasino has taught me about the angelic tongue and that it is different from our tongues. And that the angels speak different tongues at different levels, in different choirs, Yet they all understand each other. I will tell him this.....

And what else, Father?..... About the different plateaus in the kingdom and how people should strive to get to the highest plateau. I will tell him about what takes place in the kingdom. What they have to look forward to, and what they will find..... I'll do that, Father..... I will tell him about the saints, and the duties of the saints. Even though they're with the Father, how they help us and watch over us..... And I will tell him the true role of Mary as a loving, sweet, wonderful mother..... I will tell him, Father, of Your gentleness and of your love. And how you want us to respond to You as a child.....

There is so much that You want me to say, Father..... No. I will say everything that You want me to say..... **Grace.** You helped me with a tape about that, Father. I will tell them the essentials of grace..... My mind doesn't click as fast as yours, Father. You forget who You're dealing with. You're dealing with a dummy..... (laughs) Father, I love You, but You just can't push aside that I'm not so bright..... If You say so..... You know, for awhile I forgot about that "grace of anticipation." That will come under "grace," Father. I will tell them about that, because sometimes people think, "Well, it's too late to pray, because they're dead." They don't know about the "grace of anticipation." I will reveal it to them, my Father.....

See, I really need to write this stuff down, Father. I know, and I think of that grace often, but then, that's it. It slips away until I need it again. I will tell them these things.

And what else do You want me to tell them, my Father..... **The cycle of love.** I know! Falling in love with Butchie, and He leads to the Father. And falling deeply in love with the Father. And then the Father leads to the Holy Spirit..... **They must know of this cycle.....** They speak of baptism in the Spirit. I go by what You say, my Father..... **They must learn about this mystical cycle. It's mystical and there's no other way.....** I understand. But see, I didn't give that another thought. I know it, but I don't stop to teach it.....

Your mind is perfect, so that's why You remember..... **I must tell them about the intimacy there is in the Eucharist. The consummation of love is the Eucharist. Bone of Your bone. Flesh of Your flesh.....** I'll tell them, Father, everything Thomasino has taught me, and what You have taught me..... **About when Butchie was little.** I'll have to remember that, Father. If You please, would You refresh my memory. I forget so much..... Whatever You say. Father, I love You. You're not tiring me at all. You know You're not. I'm just so delighted, but I'm hoping You'll let me remember through the Spirit. You've given me so much, and my mind is so weak..... Maybe I am underestimating it. But I don't underestimate the Spirit for sure.....

As You give me titles, I will write them down. And You will fill me with the revelations I need for that title..... Yes, Father..... **And all the prophecies and all the revelations.** Whatever You wish..... I don't think You've laid a heavy burden on me..... Where there is love, there is no burden. You told me that Yourself, my Father..... I love You too, and that makes everything worthwhile..... Nope. I see their faces so excited with hope and expectation.....

INTERVIEW

I noticed, Eileen, that the Father seemed very happy this time.
My Father? Sure he was.
And you were happy to see Him so happy.
He was beaming and His eyes were dancing. Sometimes His
eyes look glossy when He cries. He cries for His people. But He
was so happy, so beautiful, so handsome. Just perfect.
What made Him so happy? Because You're sharing?
He's happy because my services went right and I listened to
the Spirit. He's happy because I revealed some of the kingdom to
the people in the Sunday talk, and they were relishing it, and they're
talking about it. He's happy because the diocese is beginning to
stir because of my talks, and the priests being at the talks. They're
talking about it to others. At St. Mary's in Jefferson, there were
about eight priests there. He said they're beginning to talk about
it. He said that this is what He wanted, to stir up the diocese. He's
very happy.
So, there was a lot of hope and expectation?
Yes, and He's happy because I did so well. He knew the services were difficult. They were very difficult. Sunday I said, "What
am I going to talk about? I'm all talked out." And then I got sick.
But my Father said, "Just trust in Me and the words will come."
And He was happy because I felt like backing out of the divorce
group. I felt like backing out of St. Mary's. They came to my Sunday
service *[at St. John's]*, and they said it was the best service I ever
gave, so my Father was happy.
And Butchie was very tender.
Oh, He was tender and loving and mushy. (laughs)
What did He say when you said that the whole world doesn't
see the ring?
Oh, He was fascinated by my wedding ring. And I said, "The

world doesn't see it." And He said, "It's not meant for them. It's meant for Me." And You know what He said? I can bilocate in the kingdom. See, I'm His bride. I belong to Butchie. In the kingdom I can go to His plateau as His bride. And it will be just He and me on that plateau. It is a special plateau for His bride. This is what He's doing. It's amazing. I won't have to share Him with anybody that I know about.

He has a number of others who are truly brides.

Well, I don't know where they're going. That's their business, and I don't want to know about it. But I know where I'm going. I'll be with Him. Do you understand?

Yes. You asked the Father to tell you again. You said, "You told me two minutes ago, but I want to hear it again." And then He told you and you said, "Thank You, Father."

How much He loves me. And how much He's going to use me. He said, "Do you know how much I love You, Eileen, and how much You mean to me?" I said, "I know, but I'd like to hear it some more." I love to hear him say it because He squeezes me and kisses me and loves me.

And then He said He wants you to tell somebody everything. You.

And then He said something about when Butchie was little, and you said, "Refresh my memory."

About all the things we used to do.

19. A NEW LIGHT HAS BEEN SENT TO GOD'S PEOPLE
October 5, 1983

I'm listening, Father.

(repeating the Father's words)

You will shine as a beacon light before all men, and you will bring your Father's words to them. And they will know that you have been lifted up by the Father. It is not by chance that you are here or there, but by the Father's will. A new light has been sent to God's people and it will light up the whole world.

That's wonderful, Father, but I hope I don't let You down. I wouldn't want to let You down, Father.

20. THE REVOLUTION OF LOVE IN THE CHURCH
November 12, 1983

There is so much peace here. I don't want to shut out the problems of the world, Butchie, but it seems as though we always have to bring these problems here lately, and discuss them..... I don't really know, Butchie. I think it's because we haven't been taught about the kingdom..... Yes, we know the Commandments. But we haven't been taught the joys, the things to expect in holy expectation. Just the cut and dry fundamentals.....

Oh, Butchie, I can't do that by myself..... Well I know, but I need some humans to help me, too..... Nope, I don't think I'm overburdening the Spirit, that's His job..... Where do I begin, and how far do I go, Butchie? Where do I end?..... **I end in the Father's arms.** But what's in between?..... I guess now is as good a time as any..... I let them know a little. I just can't tell them everything, Butchie. I think it would be too much for them to grasp. Don't You think so?.....

They did love it. But, Butchie, if I tell them all the beauty that's here in its majesty, can they grasp it? Will they understand? Even some of my priests don't understand..... If that's what You wish, I'll do it, and I'm sure the Spirit will enlighten me. I'll do whatever the Spirit wants..... I know there's trouble, Butchie. But how can You bring them to the reality of something they can't see, feel or touch?..... Well, I hope they'll listen.....

They'll say, "How do you know so much, and what book did you get that from, and where does it say that in Scripture?" What am I going to say? It's not there..... I don't think they'll buy that..... Yes, they know me..... Yep, they know what I stand for..... **Then they'll believe.....** I hope. If you say they will, they will. **This is the hour that we must reveal, not only the Father, but the kingdom to the Father's children, so they'll hunger and thirst after it. And in** thirsting after it, they'll hunger and thirst after the Lord, our God. That's quite a big order, Butchie..... Are they really thirsting after truth, or do they just want to know the other side of the coin, no matter what it is.....

I'll give them truth. Because You taught it to me, Butchie, and the Father teaches me..... I'm sure the Spirit will lead me.....

I said there are two revolutions in the Church. The anti-Roman Catholic revolution and the revolution of the charismatic movement, a revolution of love working within the Church.....

I don't remember that..... Oh, yes I do. I said the Father, because He's so just and righteous and merciful, is balancing the revolution in the Church with the revolution of love of the charismatic movement, as long as it's subject to the authority of the Church. And this is the Father's way of balancing it and giving us a chance..... But who'll win out?..... That's a mission for sure..... That's a big order. I don't even want to face those students, never mind this..... Of course I love You and of course I trust You..... Nope. You'll never leave me. As long as we pull together we can do it.

Is the revolution really bad, Butchie? I know the Father talks of it often..... Bet He's real sad about it, hey?..... You can make excuses for the laity, but I can't for them. They know where it's at, and they're our teachers..... Butchie, they know that they're subject to the temptations of the world and they should make use of prayer, virtue, obedience. They're falling right into it..... It's getting worse. I see it with the priests and the sisters. I wish there were some way I could hide it from the Father, but He sees everything.....

See, that's what I mean, Father. You probably wouldn't get so hurt if You didn't keep nosing around the corners. Then you get hurt. See, You want to know everything. If You stop knowing some stuff, then You wouldn't be so sad..... I was talking to Butchie, and You were listening..... I won't give You twenty lashes, I'll give You twenty kisses. But I don't like You to be hurt, Father. You listen to everything..... Butchie said the revolution was getting worse in the Church. In dealing with priests, I know it for sure..... Well, just do what Butchie says, start a revolution of love, and we'll win out. Love for the Father, for the Church. Then will come love for each other. And in this love there's submission and obedience.....

(laughs) I guess it is a big cup of tea. You're stealing my expressions, Father..... You don't even have tea here..... Butchie said I must reveal Your kingdom. He said my job is to reveal the Father, but also the kingdom, and what they are to get, and to expect. So they will desire it more and crave for it more. My Father, how can I reveal everything You have revealed to me? Will they grasp it?..... How can I do that?..... **Bribe them. Whet their desires.....** Oh, You mean like the plateaus..... Are they really thinking about it? (laughs) There'll be a scramble for the seventh plateau.....

Will You help me to whet their desires?..... (laughs) In my next talk? Their desires will be for the turkey on the table..... You're not supposed to talk like that, You sound like a gangster..... (laughs) I'll tell them Father God says we've got to talk turkey today, so we're going to talk about Heaven..... (laughs) You're funny. I love You so much. I love it when You laugh and act funny. I just love it so much. You are so light and so beautiful. I hate to see you so heavily burdened.

You know what really gets me, Father, if You knew all this was going to happen, why did You make us?..... That would be an awful, powerful, deep and heavy teaching..... Yes, I think so. I know so..... Oh, because I have people telling me, "Oh, God knows where I'm going, so what does it matter.".... But would they understand this? And could I put this across? It's awful deep, my Father. You better repeat it again, and tell the Holy Spirit to help me.....

You mean like Adam and Eve. **You knew that they were going to eat the apple.** See it isn't a fable, it's truth. Right, Father? It is truth. There was an Adam and an Eve, and there was an apple.

You know what I heard the other day? That it wasn't an apple at all. A priest told me it was sex. And I told him what my Father said, sex was beautiful in the Garden and they participated in it and there was no sin in it, until they ate the forbidden fruit, and then they began to find it something sinful and to cover themselves. They put the sin in it, not the Father.....

What are you asking me for? You were there. You would know if he dug it. I think he did. Do you think he did?..... (laughs) You are so silly. I don't know why You ask me questions, my Father, when You know all the answers..... (laughs) Don't do that, oh, Father. It feels warm...... Nope. Almost yummy. But I want to think of what I'm doing. I've got You now, and I want to ask You all these questions..... I know You're never too busy, and I like to ask.....

See, You're trying to distract me. I love You, but I want to know all about this stuff. So Adam and Eve is not a fable. There was really an apple, and these theologians are barking up the wrong tree. They're just twisting things around, right?..... **Right.** But You knew they were going to eat that fruit. You're God. You know everything. So You could have avoided it..... **Free will.** There we go again..... So, You knew they were going to do it, so what did You do about it..... **Jesus.** There goes balance again.....

So, how do You balance this? You knew there was going to be a revolution in the Church, why didn't You stop it? Now how are You going to balance this one off?..... **Grace and acceptance of grace. Jesus there again. So You won't stop it, but You'll draw good from it.** That's pretty deep. Especially when I know You're God and You know everything. You see what it is, my Father, we're human, and we find it so hard, Father, to understand free will. We have to know more about this free will, this wonderful but dangerous gift You have given us. It's wonderful. It's beautiful to the point that it can get us into Heaven, into the kingdom, with the right decisions and acceptance of grace, Father. But it's dangerous, because we can go the other way with it. We have to know more about this one, Father, and how You don't interfere with it. It's up to us.....

An airplane. I guess You would call it a chance..... But in my free will I bought it, and if it blows up, or goes down, You don't stop it, because it was my free will that allowed me to buy it..... I see. My Father, what You say is truth. But would they accept it from me?..... This whole revolution in the Church has started from the free will..... (laughs) I don't mean to look grim, my Father. No way. Love me all You want..... (laughs)

INTERVIEW

He was giving You a lot of loving?

I felt just like a sponge. Porous and absorbing it all. I didn't want to miss any of it. (laughs)

Well, you're learning how to accept love.

He pours it and I absorb it. (laughs) He told me He wanted to squeeze me. I said, Don't squeeze me too tight. I don't want to lose any of it. (laughs) The reason He gave me so much loving, His teachings were heavy.

You were talking about Adam and Eve and the apple and that priest. You said the Father would know whether the priest accepted the explanation you gave?

Right. He said, "Did he accept it?" I said, "You don't miss anything. Why are you asking me, You were there." He laughed. He likes to hear it from me. See, if I don't have to tell Him anything because He was there, we're not going to grow deeper in love. By sharing we do. Many times He'll say, "Eileen, I was there, but I want to hear it from you. That's conversation and we grow deeper in love with each other."

That explains prayer.

Yep.

He said you could give Him twenty lashes? You said I'll give You twenty kisses. Remember that?

I forgot how He put it. I said, "They're not going to be listening to revelation, they're going to be thinking of their Thanksgiving turkeys." He said, "You know what we're going to do, Eileen, we're going to talk turkey to them." He is so funny. I said, "Father, You're so silly." (laughs) He said, "Well, we're going to talk turkey to them. We're going to get this message across."

What did He say when you said, "You don't have tea up here?"

He laughed. I'm always saying that's a big cup of tea. They don't have tea there. They have something better than tea. They have something better than coffee. See, Heaven is everything we desire, only more so. He prepared all this beautiful stuff we love down here that's kosher and good before Him. But Heaven is all this beautiful stuff but creamier, better than we can imagine.

When you asked Him would they grasp it, revealing Heaven to them, He said: "Bribe them"?

Yes, like when I was talking about the different plateaus, they went crazy. They love it. They're hungry to know this stuff. They have never heard it before, and when they hear it, their ears go almost to a point, like a donkey's ears. You can tell they're listening, their eyes are big. They want to know about the kingdom.

So that's another thing in your mission, to reveal the kingdom to the people. He said you could reveal everything that He revealed to you?

Only in spots. You know I can't give them everything at once.

You told Him they'll say, "Well, it's not in Scripture, how do you know this?" And He said, "They'll believe you. "

Yes, and He said, "They have up until now, Eileen, and they're hungering for it. They love you, they respect you, they know you stand on firm ground." He said it's time to give them the revelations of the Father.

And He said as time goes on they're going to understand what a revelation is. It's God revealing to them His kingdom.

When you were talking about those two revolutions, He said that the revolution of love would win out?

He said there is a great revolution in the Church. Disobedience, indifference, not following doctrine and tradition. Especially disobedience. But He said He gave the charismatic movement, a movement of love provided it's within the Church, to blossom and suppress this.

It's still going to do that, the charismatic movement?

If they work within the Church. You know, they're not working too much within the Church.

But He has hopes for the charismatic movement?

Yes, because it's a movement of the Holy Spirit. But, it works outside the Church too. L's girl friend said, "I love your services but I don't want to hear about doctrine." I said, "Well, if you don't you're in trouble. There's something wrong there and you better find out what it is." The letters I get in the mail, people are just so proud to be Roman Catholics. And the people in New York, they just stand up. *[Eileen speaks in her services of being proud that we are Roman Catholics. Her mail indicates that people are responding positively to this.]* And that's what we've got to get back to.

You said the mission that He is giving you is a big order?

Did you read that article where they're going to look deeper into the teachings of Martin Luther? My Father said looking deeper into it, they'll find some sound teaching, but we're also almost going to approve of his disobedience, and that shouldn't be done.

He said we'd find some sound teaching?

He said he knew his stuff. But besides that, we're going to see he disobeyed and yet he's being acknowledged as a great man. So my Father said they're going to have a battle there. They're not going to look at the disobedience, they're going to look at the "great man." But my Father doesn't approve of that.

He wouldn't mind their looking into his doctrine deeper, if they also looked into and admitted the disobedience?

Right,. They've got to admit the disobedience to the Church. He was far from a humble man.

What was the big order that He gave you and you said, "It's bad enough to try to face the students, let alone this." What did He want you to do?

He wanted me to talk about the revolution in the Church.

To your people in your services?

To my people. But He also wants me to lift up the revolution of love that should be starting in the Roman Catholic Church. True love for God and for the Church, and our human love *[love for one another]* will come with it, and then we'll be subject to authority. He said all the preaching in the world isn't going to get us back to the right path. It's the love we can give each other.

What answer did Butchie give you when you said you need humans to help you?

He said "God made Adam and Eve human and they caused chaos in the world, so why shouldn't the Father use humans to bring back peace." But they have to be subject to the Spirit.

21. ADVENT: THE WELL
December 11, 1983

[During Advent Eileen is in desolation and aridity. From this "well"
she calls the Father.]

I am relaxed here..... It's a different world here, Butchie.....

I feel His love and His warmth. It takes away the dullness. I think it *[the well]* is a valuable place to be and an important place to be. Nobody can get to me here. I can think about my Father and about Your love..... I know He's here. In the solitude I call for the Father. If He doesn't answer I call some more. My heart beats faster hoping to hear His voice, hoping to hear a creak to know He's here. The desire grows so strong, it burns my very soul.

Not that I like being here, but I like the feeling of wanting Him so much and loving Him so much and needing Him so much. I want to call out for sure, and yet the desire of wanting Him, that actually brings peace to my soul.

At one time I thought I was going to get out and I was almost hoping I would slip back, so I could desire Him and call Him and crave Him. I was almost afraid that if I found Him that wonderful desire would be gone. Do You understand what I am saying? I can't explain it, but there is such joy in seeking Him, such peace, heart-break yes, but such peace. I can't explain it.

When was that?..... In the Garden of Olives. It was like being in the well. You were seeking Him and searching for Him. But He wouldn't answer You..... I'm just amazed. I don't know what to say. I would never have compared my experience to that.

22. THE CHILD
   December 21, 1983

But I understand some of it now..... (coughs) I can write that in my little notebook..... **As soon as Mary laid eyes upon You, You looked up at Mary, and deep loved flowed.** So You could see..... I think that's beautiful..... There's so much more that we don't know, Butchie. I'm not one for digging into things, but we're missing so many beautiful things about You, Mary and Joseph, the carpenter, the faithful husband of Mary.....

  I'm very glad You showed it to me. I truly love You as a child, as a baby, but I can't relate too much to You that way, because I didn't know You as a baby..... I told You, it's like looking at baby pictures in an album. You're very beautiful and You're very special, and You're eyes are very wise. You can almost see the whole world in Your face..... Oh, sure. Who can resist a baby?.....

  Butchie, there is such conflict about how much You knew, how much You didn't know. It really doesn't matter to me, but what You're revealing to me is really something great. **You had wisdom and knowledge and understanding of who You were and of Your Father. But You went along at the pace Mary expected You to go.....** I understand what You're telling me..... I think it would be difficult, but You're saying it wasn't difficult for You. I know You're the Son of the Father..... Then, You could have walked but You didn't until Mary expected You to walk, right?..... But when she expected You to do things, that's when You did them.....

  I'm just amazed because, to tell You the truth, Butchie, I never went into this. I've heard people wonder how much You knew. Like when You were in the Temple, if You knew or if You didn't know, and it didn't really bother me, and I never really gave it much thought. But now that You're telling me this, of course I'm amazed, and I think it's great You're telling me.....

What·a comparison that is! **A real dirty child and a real clean child.** Of course the dirty child knows he's shabby and dirty, and the clean child knows he's all clean and appealing. **You knew You were all good and all holy, a child of the Father. It wouldn't be right if You didn't know it.** When You put it that way, I can understand it. I don't know if the world can understand it. But You've given me the grace to understand it, and I take Your word for it..... I think that's super.....

I don't know how much of it they would grasp. They might think I'm a dodo. I can't say, "Butchie told me." Then I'd get it with both barrels..... Well, I understand what You're saying, and it sits very right with me. It must have been a beautiful life..... When you present Yourself to me as a child in the manger, I'm wondering how You can be here beside me and at the same time I look down and see You there..... I think it's beautiful, and now You'll have more meaning for me.

I think it's super of You telling me all this..... Nope, I didn't think it was a myth. No way. When they said there was a donkey there, and the sheep and the animals, of course I believed there were..... **You knew they were there, and You could feel their breath warming You. And You weren't afraid?..... Fear comes from sin. You had no sin, there was no fear in You.** That's right..... I keep forgetting, Butchie, but I'm glad You're refreshing my memory....

Often as I kneel before Your image in the Church or when I'm on the sofa, I wondered just what was going on..... **You didn't think it was a dumpy place. You thought it was neat.....** How could You think it was neat? Look where You came from. The valley, the plateaus..... **It was neat because the animals were friendly, and Mary and Joseph loved each other and loved You.** There it is.....

Nope. Scripture said the Magi came..... Some say it is a myth. Is it true, Butchie?..... **They brought You gifts.** Were You aware of this as an infant?..... **Aware, but not noticeably aware.....** It wasn't a myth. It really happened. Tell me more about them, Butchie. I don't know anything about them..... But how could they be touched by grace? You hadn't died yet to acquire grace for them..... **The goodness of their God.** Would that be a natural grace not a supernatural one? And if they knew that the star meant something, then how could they follow it without being inspired by the Spirit who hadn't come to the people yet? You better make it clear to me, Butchie, I don't understand this..... **They couldn't be aware of this if they didn't have special light.....** Did the Father speak to them? Could they hear?..... **In their hearts they heard.** But Moses heard *[God speaking to him]*..... **They didn't hear aloud.** I understand that kind *[that is, God speaking in the heart]*.....

I think it's kind of deep..... It isn't? Well make it clearer, then. **The Father spoke to them in their own tongue so they would understand that they must seek this child out.....** And then what happened?..... **They brought the best gifts of their land.....** I think more people should know this, Butchie..... I'm not going to tell them. I'm not talking about nothing..... I think it's just very beautiful..... Nope, I'm thrilled to death. It means so much more to me.....

And they understood the love of the Father and of the Christ Child. You, Butchie..... Nope. I don't mean to look confused. I'm still wondering where they got the grace. I understand natural grace and natural goodness. Then, they didn't get the grace that You won from the cross?..... Aha! **The grace of anticipation. The Father knew they were coming. He knew You were going to die. Some of the graces You acquired by Your death were applied to the Magi.** I remember the truck driver..... Then that's a very important grace, right, Butchie?.....

Why didn't You tell all the writers this instead of a dumbhead? I can't do anything. But I love it. I love it for sure, and I'm excited about the manger now..... You have so many secrets. I'm so happy You're sharing them with me, Butchie..... I'm delighted. I think

it's wonderful You're telling me this right now, in this season.....
Oh sure, it picks me up, because I miss my Father, You know.....
People wouldn't want to hear that. It sounds only logical. It makes
me see how the Father really loves the animals and why I love them
so much because I'm His kid. And why there's no eating of meat
in Heaven..... I understand. **Because it would be destroying life.** I
understand..... I understand so much more now about the manger
and about that grace *[the Magi had]*.....It's a very powerful grace.....
And a lot of good came from the crucifixion even before the crucifixion..... I think it's real neat, and I think it shows how much You
and the Father love us. He thinks of all the answers. He thinks of
ever so many ways to save us and to draw us closer to Himself, and
that makes me love Him even more, if that's at all possible.....

I know You do, Butchie..... Oh sure..... That's not too many
days..... Of course I mind being there *[in the well]*, and yet, I truly
know the joy that I feel there. It blows my mind that one can be at
two different levels at the same time, almost a contradiction. So
sad and empty and yet so full of joy. And I think of what You told
me about the Garden *[of the agony]*..... There is so much about
You that we don't know, Butchie..... Well, why don't You reveal it
to these smart guys so that they can do something about it.....

INTERVIEW

Butchie saw His mother as soon as He was born? She looked
at Him and He looked at her?

You were listening again.

Yes.

He told me a lot of secrets. He said He had wisdom and knowledge.

Did He say that He saw His Father the way He sees Him now?

Yes. He saw my Father. He only went at the pace that Mary

expected Him to move, and that the neighbors expected. He could have gotten up and walked. He knew what was going on. He knew many, many things. He said the thing that keeps us from knowledge is original sin. Or else we would have been born with infused knowledge. That's our blockage. Sin keeps babies from not seeing. It's an imperfection. But He didn't have any imperfections.

He knew He was the Son of God right from the start?

Oh, He knew He was the Son of God right from the beginning. He revealed His knowledge at the pace Mary expected. She knew, and she was watching for outstanding things, and He was alert to what she was watching for. Mary knew He was the Son of God. She knew He was brilliant from the beginning, and she was watching for His fast moves, but He wouldn't make any fast moves.

He wouldn't rush things?

No.

He hid all that He had and just responded as a child would normally?

She knew though. She knew that He knew. She knew His brightness. She wanted to see if He was going to walk at three months instead of twelve or eleven, and He knew it, but He wasn't going to do it. And He walked when any normal child would be expected to walk. Maybe a little before.

How about Joseph?

He said Joseph was watching for all the signs too.

He knew too?

Oh, he knew, and he had many secrets tucked away in his heart, Butchie said. When Joseph was teaching Him to do things, Joseph knew He knew, but he watched His docility in learning. Jesus pretended He was learning. Jesus was a master in whatever Joseph taught. And Joseph knew. But He'd only go at the pace Joseph was taking Him. Because He was the Son of God, He could do it. We'd say, "I know how to do this." But not He. Isn't that something?

Yes. So He was there with you and then . . .

He was alongside of me, and we were looking at Him in the manger.

And He was just like He was when He was in the manger? This is real?

Yes, but I couldn't relate to Him.

Did your heart go out to Him at all?

Of course it did. I love babies. You know I love babies.

Yes. But I don't mean as a baby but as a spouse.

It was like looking at a picture album. It's hard to believe Butchie was there. Like looking at His baby pictures.

And He liked the cave?

He said it was beautiful because the animals were peaceful, and there was nothing but love there. Mary and Joseph were very much in love and they were in awe of the baby. He said, "That's what Heaven's all about, why shouldn't I love it? I didn't feel poor, I felt wealthy." He loved it there because there was nothing but love. And Mary and Joseph didn't feel bad that their son was born in a manger, because they were all pure and everything was beautiful. The hay was beautiful, the animals were beautiful. They didn't feel sadness in their hearts. They were happy.

Did He say whether the animals took to Him too?

Well, He said that they breathed upon Him and kept Him warm. And He said that's why He doesn't — You eat everything in Heaven, but you don't find meat there. You don't even find fish there. All kinds of fruits and breads and stuff, but you don't find any fish or any meat there. Never. I haven't anyway.

He said there is no killing of animals in Heaven?

There is so much we don't know. I wonder why we don't know anything.

But as a baby He looked pretty wise, you could see the wisdom in His eyes?

Yes, the wisdom. His eyes were bright and sparkly. Alert. Just to look at Him you knew He's special.

And the love?

Yes, just to look at Him.

But did He look at you from His eyes as a baby?

He looked right at me with Butchie's eyes.

With love?

Beautiful love. I'm amazed at Mary and Joseph thinking the manger was just a magnificent place for Him. They don't look at things like we do. There was love, and there was peace. And there was that prayer, that holiness between them. When you have all that you don't need mansions. We people are so funny. He taught me a lot.

And He told you about the Magi coming?

They're saying it's myth. I heard priests saying it this past week, and on television, too. The Father said, "No, Eileen, it wasn't a myth." But I couldn't understand how they could be touched by grace to come [to seek Jesus] when Jesus had not yet died to give them that grace. But there is a grace of anticipation. He knew He was going to die and said I'm giving them the grace. He said the Father spoke to their hearts. They didn't hear His voice coming from the heavens, like Moses: a loud, loud voice. But the Father spoke to their hearts. They knew what they heard was from God, and they followed it, and they came.

But wasn't there a star that led them?

A star led them. Butchie knew I was upset over it, because the priest said, "No, that's myth. It was a planet." And my Father said, "No, that star was never there until I put it there. And that was when Christ was [to be] born. It's not myth." He said, "I don't care what they tell you, Eileen, don't believe it." You should hear the stories now about the Christ Child, you wouldn't believe it. And Butchie said, "No. They want everything to be a myth, but it's true."

And they brought Him gifts?

They brought Him what was the wealthiest thing in their land. And it was the frankincense and myrrh and all this. That was the wealthiest thing they had in their land.

Were they priests?

I don't know. The Father never said they were priests. They were very holy men. Good men. They were in awe when they came. They knew He was special. They felt that there was something in the air that was different. They knew. And that was grace. And I said, "Butchie, how could they be touched by grace?" And He said, "Eileen, it was the grace of anticipation." Butchie told me about a truck driver that got killed.

I remember that. You said a rosary for him.

And He brought it back to me. He said, "Eileen, your rosary saved that man." I said, "Butchie, how could my rosary save him, he was already dead?" He said, "I knew from the beginning of time, you were going to say that rosary, and I applied that grace *[at the time of his death. At the moment of the accident he cried out: 'My Jesus, have mercy!']*" See how wonderful our Father is. He finds every loophole.

So He gave them grace from Butchie's sacrifice?

From what He said, they were good men, really good men. Each one was from a different place. The Father spoke to their hearts and they knew it was the Father, so they had to have some kind of grace to know the Father's voice. And then, when they saw Butchie, they were overwhelmed with love and grace. I said, "Butchie, how could they recognize You?" They recognized Him. They knew He was special. And to know He's special, that was grace.

Now what is natural grace?

The Father calls it natural goodness. If a person is naturally good, the Father calls his goodness natural grace. It's natural. It could be inherited. There is so much we don't know about Jesus.

And His childhood is one of the most beautiful parts of His life.

And what is this about Moses? How did He speak to Moses?

Well, He spoke from the heavens. Loud and clear. Moses heard His voice.

They talked face to face.

He speaks in different ways. Sometimes the Father speaks through a voice in your heart. You hear Him but you can't see Him. You don't hear Him with your ears. You hear Him with the ears of the soul as clear as anything. There is no other way I can explain it. At other times, He speaks in a loud voice. He'll say, "Eileen." I'll say, "Yes, Father." And there He is. Sometimes He speaks and I can't see Him, and sometimes He speaks and I see Him.

Which do you like best? Which way of His speaking to you?

I like all ways. He speaks differently to my heart. But naturally I love when He speaks to me and I can see Him.

But isn't that very intimate when He speaks to your heart?

I don't know. I like to see Him in front of me or by my side, and I like to be at His knees. I like that very much. You forget I'm still human. I'm not satisfied with that inner stuff yet. (laughs) I love it though. Love it. I know He's there.

INDEX

Holy Year 22
Host 11
hunger for God 16
hungry for the word 15

I

identity, Eileen's. *See* Eileen's
    identity
illness
    Eileen's 131, 135. *See also*
        suffering: Eileen's
illness (cancer)
    Eileen's, not healed 136

J

Jesus(') 11
    appearing on the altar
        Eileen's desire 73, 76, 80
    ascent to His Father 51. *See
        also* souls, holy
    cross 33, 36. *See also* cross, the
    death
        for the per-
            son 26, 31, 33, 36
    descent into Hell 51
    from infancy on did things
        (e.g.) walking, at expected
        time 167, 170
    His wisdom and knowl-
        edge 167
    knew He was Son of Father
        and all holy 168, 171
    in infancy
        His eyes 173
        saw the Father 170
    in manger

        thought it a neat place 168
        not afraid 168
        with donkey and ox, not a
            myth 168
    knowing 49, 53
    knowledge and abilities he did
        not show 171
    Magi brought gifts, not a
        myth 168
    robes, odor 113
    suffering 32, 33, 36, 42
    when a child 154
Joan of Arc 78, 81
    sent to Eileen 77
Joseph
    knew Jesus was a master,
        watched His docility 171

K

Kim, Stephen Cardinal 7

L

Lent 34
    withdrawal 60
liberals 73, 78, 79, 81, 137. *See
    also* Church: "the fallen away
    Church"
    doing an awful job on the
        Church 82
lies travel fast 45, 49
"Life in the Spirit" 46, 49
light
    a new 142, 157
    to the Church 108
light, the
    in the valley 109

Eileen's books, audiotapes and videotapes may be obtained from
the Meet-The-Father Ministry
363 Greenwood Street
Millbury, MA 01527

Eileen George: Beacon of God's Love: Her Teaching

Eileen George's Conversations in Heaven

Eileen George's Conversations in Heaven II

$10 each. Add $2.50 for shipping and handling for the first book,
$1.25 for each additional book to the same address.

Eileen's "The Father's Good News Letter" may be obtained free
of charge on request.

For video and audio tapes, write for catalog.